P9-DZZ-712

More praise for Nancy Pine's *Educating Young Giants*

"This is a lively, informative book that covers a wide range of pressing educational questions by a wise educator with extensive experience studying teaching and learning in both China and the United States. It is loaded with vivid descriptions based on first-hand experience of dramatic differences in how Chinese and American parents and teachers approach the task of educating contemporary children."

—Joseph Tobin, The Hall Professor of Education, University of Georgia, and author of *Preschool in Three Cultures Revisited: China, Japan, and the United States*

"Dr. Pine has spent twenty years studying educational practices in classrooms throughout China and the United States with observant eyes, clarity of description, and insight that allows us to see what we have not seen before: the strengths and challenges of each system. The brilliance of Pine's book exemplifies how educators in China and the United States can learn from and with each other in an international professional community that she has nurtured throughout her career. This book is for academics in universities and practitioners in classrooms, school districts, and state departments of education."

—Dr. Christelle Estrada, Secondary English Language Arts Specialist, Utah State Office of Education

"*Educating Young Giants* is a delightfully written book geared toward educators that is fully accessible to the general public and policymakers. From detailed observations and interviews based on 30 different visits to China over roughly the past quarter-century, Nancy Pine charts an education-reform future relevant to both countries. *Educating Young Giants* is an essential and enjoyable read for anyone who cares about education."

—Richard Shavelson, Chief Research Officer, SK Partners, LLC, and Margaret Jacks Professor of Education, Emeritus, Stanford University

"A fascinating book about teaching, learning, and the contrasting styles of the Chinese and U.S. education and cultural systems. Pine finds a way to highlight the best features of each system from a deep, practical understanding of both, offering a pathway for global collaboration in the twentieth century. Whether you are a parent or an educator, you will find this book difficult to put down. Neither China nor the

U.S. can afford to ignore or put aside the concepts brought forth in Pine's fascinating book about the underpinnings of the educational and cultural systems of both countries."

—Louis Carrillo, Elementary School Principal, Los Angeles
Unified School District

"*Educating Young Giants* is an important book, especially for all concerned people in China and the United States, in which the author, based on a twenty-year ongoing study, compares and contrasts the educational systems of the two most important countries in the world today."

—Thayer Scudder, Professor of Anthropology Emeritus,
California Institute of Technology

"This is quite a remarkable book that should be required reading for students preparing to become teachers, for practicing teachers, and also for educational leaders and policy makers engaged in educational reform. The author, Nancy Pine, brings her extensive experiences in education in the U.S. and China to the comparison of teaching and learning in these two countries. But this is not a standard academic study or a simple contrast and therein lies its strength. Nancy is a skillful writer and has used detailed colorful descriptions of her many observations of classrooms and conversations with educators to allow us to see what she saw and hear what she heard. In a strikingly unbiased and non-judgmental way, she reflects on these stories drawing from the literature and her deep knowledge of the history and cultures of both countries to deepen her own understanding and enrich ours."

—Karen Worth, Instructor, Department of Elementary Education,
Wheelock College; Consultant in Science Education

"For those who have not lived in or experienced firsthand education in the U.S. or China, this book brings important insights into the way parents and teachers educate their children in both countries. For readers who have worked in these two very different cultural contexts, the book provides important opportunities to reflect and will provoke lively discussions."

—Professor Tina Bruce CBE, University of Roehampton

"An invaluable contribution to the field of teacher education. *Educating Young Giants* is a fascinating comparison of the similarities and differences between the Chinese and U.S. educational systems. It should be required reading for all teacher preparation programs."

—Caryn Rossi Louie, Instructor of Chinese, North Carolina School
for Science and Mathematics and former elementary ESL teacher

Educating Young Giants

What Kids Learn (And Don't Learn) in China and America

Nancy Pine

palgrave
macmillan

KH

EDUCATING YOUNG GIANTS
Copyright © Nancy Pine, 2012.

First published in 2012 by
PALGRAVE MACMILLAN®
in the United States—a division of St. Martin's Press LLC,
175 Fifth Avenue, New York, NY 10010.

Where this book is distributed in the UK, Europe and the rest of the World,
this is by Palgrave Macmillan, a division of Macmillan Publishers Limited,
registered in England, company number 785998, of Houndmills,
Basingstoke, Hampshire RG21 6XS.

Palgrave Macmillan is the global academic imprint of the above
companies and has companies and representatives throughout the world.

Palgrave® and Macmillan® are registered trademarks in the United
States, the United Kingdom, Europe and other countries.

ISBN: 978–0–230–33906–4 (hc)
ISBN: 978–0–230–33907–1 (pbk)

Library of Congress Cataloging-in-Publication Data is available from the
Library of Congress.

A catalogue record of the book is available from the British Library.

Design by Integra Software Services

First edition: May 2012

10 9 8 7 6 5 4 3 2 1

Printed in the United States of America.

6/25/13

For
John Regan

Contents

List of Figures

Preface

December 30, 1989. I pressed my forehead against the window of Air China's Boeing 747 as it banked smoothly toward the scattered lights emerging from the darkness. A mid-career graduate student on leave from my first-grade teaching position, I was headed for China with another teacher to investigate young children's learning.

"Shanghai," I whispered.

Pushing harder against the cold glass, I began to make out mist-softened buildings and roads below. I burned with excitement, even though anxiety clawed at my stomach. What if no one was down there to meet us? Where would we stay? Our advisor had called from Shanghai two days earlier to tell us that someone would meet us at the airport. Would they really be there? We were already three hours late. It was 11 P.M. and we were penniless. Chinese money could not be bought outside the country.

When the wheels of the 747 touched the rain-washed tarmac, we turned our attention to the occasional truck and very few lights. After checking our seats for stray papers and books, we hefted our briefcases bulging with testing materials and followed the crowd into a squat gray concrete building.

An educator all my professional life, I had migrated from organizing international seminars for high school students to teaching high school English to instructing elementary school students in Pasadena, California. Now in graduate school, I wanted to dig deeper, to understand how children learn, and especially to study how different cultures embrace and support learning. When John Regan, a professor at the Claremont Graduate University and my Ph.D. advisor, asked if I would be interested in exploring these ideas in China, I could barely contain my excitement. It awakened a long-dormant desire, sparked by Chinese artifacts that populated my childhood—an embroidered work here, a tinted postcard there, and photos of mist-enshrouded mountains whose crags and silhouetted trees beckoned.

Moving as one, we passengers climbed a long set of stairs to the cage-like cubicles of Immigration Control and approached them one by one. Willing myself to look calm, I handed my passport through a small opening to the uniformed immigration officer. Expressionless, he looked carefully at it and me, then at his computer screen. I held my breath. With resounding thwacks, he stamped several papers and returned my passport with a nod. The person behind me pushed forward. I picked up my briefcase and took my first step into China.

The cavernous airport terminal echoed our progress toward the exit, where a crowd waited outside in the midnight drizzle, shivering wet. Peering through glass doors into the winter darkness, I sent a small message to whatever spirits might be listening. Let there be someone out there we recognize.

Baggage in hand, we scanned the signs that some in the crowd held up. Our names weren't on any of them. Then toward the back, I noticed a blue-jacketed arm wave tentatively, then assertively. Zhang Feng! A graduate student from Shanghai, he had been in California the previous year. His face softened with relief as we moved toward him and the other Chinese who had come to greet us.

Introductions ricocheted as we piled into a van, clouds of breath floating among us. Subdued exhilaration animated every word, every gesture. The engine turned over and, with the windows wide open, we headed into Shanghai.

Driving through the city that first night more than 20 years ago, I was struck by the differences from Los Angeles. There were no freeways with cars speeding at all hours of the night, no glitzy lights. Utilitarian trucks, vans, and bicycle lorries lumbered along rain-blackened streets past billboards advertising China's march to the future with larger-than-life washing machines, industrial gears, and new factories. We passed by a row of darkened shops, the characters on their signs a mystery. One 12-hour flight had rendered me illiterate.

In the three weeks that followed in January 1990, guided by John Regan's wise dictums about Chinese culture, we observed how children were taught and talked day and night with parents, teachers, faculty members from Nanjing universities, and recent college graduates.

We visited scores of classrooms, each packed with 50 children. Everyone wore padded leggings and jackets; it was as cold inside as out. I watched in awe as bright-eyed, black-haired youngsters focused on their teachers' rapid-fire questions and recited texts in unison at full volume. But I was appalled to see teachers criticize children in front of their classmates. "You didn't put a forehead on that girl," a teacher told a four-year-old preschooler about her drawing. A forehead? I thought.

Who would ask such a young child to think of that? I had spent time in European and Mexican schools. They were different from U.S. public schools, but nothing like this. It was the beginning of my education about Chinese teaching, with carefully choreographed lessons and classrooms resounding with loud, enthusiastic student responses. The pace was relentless.

By the end of that trip, I had found the topic for my dissertation: young children's early writing efforts in China and the United States. A year later, I returned alone to collect data in three cities spread across China. I gathered material in school after school, spent hours with colleagues and a growing number of friends, and rode endless miles on coal-burning trains with chain-smoking cadres, curious families, and farmers. Since then I have made more than 30 trips to China, each time deepening my understanding of its system of education and its 4,000-year-old culture, so different from the schools and variegated cultural landscape of the United States.

*   *   *   *   *

Education is my passion, and comparing how Chinese and American children learn has become something of an obsession for me. From Lanzhou in western Gangsu Province to Fushan, northeast of Beijing, I've observed lessons and talked with teachers and parents. For whatever reason, I've connected with these people and they with me—a bond that only continues to deepen. Nearly two-dozen years after that first flight to Shanghai, I still travel to China frequently to coordinate exchange programs, consult, continue research, and always to learn more. Over a period of several years beginning in 2004 I spent three months in a rural village, learning about its history, the barriers to getting equitable education opportunities for the children, and how villagers try to solve these problems.

My understanding of Chinese classrooms has become more textured and refined with time, as has my grasp of how U.S. and Chinese classrooms compare. Each insight about Chinese educational perspectives helps me see American schooling in new ways. I understand how important polished lessons and detailed knowledge of subjects are in China, as well as the toll exacted by exam pressure. And I have come to realize that U.S. schooling, in spite of its increasing reliance on narrow tests, encourages students to express independent ideas. I've studied how children learn to write Chinese characters, what we can learn from cross-cultural misunderstandings, and how respect is shown between teacher and student, parent and child. I've loved immersing myself in conversations about what I am learning, both when I'm in China and when I return to the United States, and the ongoing exploration of the similarities and differences in our educational systems.

My research partner from China Women's University in Beijing and I currently study teaching and learning in urban and rural elementary schools. In the United States, I direct a program that connects Mount St. Mary's College in Los Angeles with China through visiting scholars, email dialogues, and a student exchange program. Previously, I'd run the college's elementary education program, instructing both beginning and experienced teachers. My colleagues and friends at Nanjing University, some of whom I met on that first trip in the winter of 1989–1990, continue to be touchstones, answering my myriad questions and helping me understand the nuances of their culture and traditions.

I still do not speak Chinese. I had studied Spanish for ten years, but when I went to China, there was no room in my life for intense language immersion. I regretted this and have since studied Chinese on and off. Although I now understand how children learn the structure of Chinese characters and how to write them, I rely on translators, interpreters, and Chinese English-speakers in research and conversation. This has provided some unexpected advantages. It has made me a student of the nonverbal, and as a result I have learned subtle behaviors in both the Chinese and my own European-American culture, perceptions I would have missed were I fluent in Chinese. Because all of my classroom observations in China are transcribed and translated, I have spent much more time perusing the intricacies of teaching methods than if I had only listened to recordings. Finally, my Chinese research partners, who are fluent in English, and I have probed at length, in deep and detailed dialogue, the misunderstandings that occur when we don't comprehend the subtleties of each others' cultures.

Educating Young Giants is for all readers who are interested in ensuring the future of our children and curious to learn about the strengths and weaknesses of Chinese and American schooling. It is also for those who seek answers to improving education in the United States so that our young people are equipped for the challenges of the twenty-first century. I hope that my experiences, thoughts, and recommendations stir your imagination.

*   *   *   *   *

Throughout the chapters in the book, I have included classroom observations drawn from decades of study. As research protocol requires, all names of students, their teachers, and schools are pseudonyms. Adult colleagues and educators, except for a few whose professions do not allow me to identify them, are referred to by their real names and identifying information. The surname of people living in China precedes their given name. When Chinese live in a Western country, they usually change the order.

Acknowledgments

First, my thanks to all my Chinese colleagues and mentors; my research partners Xu Jianyuan, Huang Ren Song, and Yu Zhenyou; to Yue Meiyun, Wen Qiufang, and An Wei; to Qiu Wei, my first research assistant who dug into many projects for me, and to the Nanjing University visiting scholars to Mount St. Mary's College: Wang Wenyu, Zhou Dandan, Yu Xi, Wang Yan, Yang Jin, Fan Hao, Liu Jiantao, Gao Qian, and Xu Lei. All have not only provided me warm hospitality but also graciously answered my myriad questions and puzzles about their culture and their schools. I hope I have done justice to their ideas and interpretations. My gratitude goes to John Regan, professor emeritus at the Claremont Graduate University, for introducing me to China and always stretching my thinking about cultural ways. This book is dedicated to him.

My appreciation also goes to the many at Mount St. Mary's College (Los Angeles) who have supported my research and interest in China over the years, and for those in the Education Department who have provided information and ideas about teaching practice. My gratitude goes to Elizabeth Campbell for her persistence in pushing me to write this book and for the steady stream of related books and articles she kept flowing my way; to my sisters, Carol and Shirley, who have been my supporters from the beginning; and to the creativity group that has sustained me for years.

My thanks also go to my agent, Carol Mann, for her belief in this book, and to Palgrave Macmillan editor, Burke Gerstenschlager, for moving it enthusiastically into publication. Without the constant help of Eric Maisel, this book might still be in its proposal form. His expert advice has been invaluable. And finally, a hearty thanks to Kris Lindgren, editor, for her way with words, and to George VanAlstine, who has read most chapters two or three times.

Most of all, my thanks and appreciation go to my family, my grown children who over the years have taught me most of what I know about learning, and to my husband, Jerry, whose enthusiasm for my work and my involvement in China have kept me wanting to learn more. Over the years, he has filled in while I have been in China, has been my first and last reader, and has enriched my ideas.

Hard Work or Natural Ability?

Watching families push through the turnstiles of the Los Angeles Zoo on a bright spring Saturday morning, I was bubbling with enthusiasm about the day of discovery ahead. I had been there dozens of times with my children and their friends, but this time I was excited for a different reason.

Zhang Feng, a Chinese friend and research colleague, and I were going to spend the morning talking about ways children learn while enjoying the animals. It was 1997. For several years, we had been studying how young children learn, but usually in short meetings during my visits to China. Now, because he was a visiting scholar to the United States, we had the luxury of an entire year to carry out research together, and I decided to show him a bit of my world while we worked.

I spotted Feng in the crowd as he walked toward the entrance. Tall for a Chinese man, he looked studious, with black-framed glasses and an overlong belt that was tucked into extra loops. In his otherwise serious face, lines along the edges of his cheeks hinted at an incipient smile. He had a flex to his walk that seemed to make it easy to lower himself to someone's eye level. I could tell from his eager stride that he was looking forward to the excursion. When I first traveled to China in 1990, we were both graduate students and we became instant friends, exploring ideas, getting to know each other's families, and probing young children's learning patterns in our two countries.

They are very different, we found.

"Let's go," I said, pushing through the turnstiles and heading up the first path. Passing the flamingoes clustered in a pond near the entrance, we joined families leaning against the fence at the prairie dog compound. Several of the little creatures sat up on hind legs looking at us, and two giggling youngsters stared back at them. A few nestled under the bushes, their dusty tan fur blending with the dirt. A mother and father discussed weekend plans while their three children watched the small animals and other things that caught their attention, like a bright umbrella one woman was using to shade herself from the sun.

As we turned to walk to the next display, Feng said with dismay, "The parents weren't talking to their children about the animals. How can they learn anything if they don't point things out to them?"

I laughed. It was Saturday, I said. They were there to relax, to enjoy the animals on a family outing. Children didn't need to be instructed all the time.

"But some of the children didn't even see the animals," Feng complained. "They were looking away or at other children, not at what they were supposed to be seeing. The parents just left the watching job for their children to figure out by themselves."

Over the years, we had often discussed our cultures' different ways of helping children understand the world around them, and we were used to being honest with each other. But Feng's comments surprised me.

"When families are relaxing," I responded, "I guess we think that the children should be able to look at what they want. I'm sure that as they go from display to display, parents will point out occasional things of interest—a polar bear swimming or a baby orangutan clinging to its mother as she climbs through branches. But not such small animals that are hard to see, unless the parent has some special interest in them."

This did not assuage him, and I was puzzled about why he felt it was important to instruct children all the time. We walked on to the sea lions and seals, through the bird aviaries, and into the large animal enclosures. As we went, he commented again that only a few parents were talking to their children about the zoo animals.

"Chinese parents would talk to their children before they got to a display, to prepare them for what to look for," he said. "Then when they arrived at the exhibit they would direct the child's sight to the animal." They would keep pointing, he added, until they were sure their child saw and understood.

How boring, I thought. There is no way I would want to be so precise about what my children saw at the zoo. They would find plenty of things to look at on their own. I might point out a few things I thought would interest them and they would no doubt ask questions about other things. I told Feng I thought we'd found one more topic to explore.

Feng and I had worked together long enough to know that when we saw things as differently as we did at the zoo, we had encountered a cultural mismatch—behaviors or habits in one society that we viewed as "wrong" or "strange" in the other. Something ingrained in his culture fought with something in mine, or vice versa—a disagreement on how each of us assumed things should be done.

This book delves deeply into those differing perspectives that Chinese and Americans have about children's learning. It excavates the cultural and historical origins of those differences and discusses their academic implications in order to arrive at an understanding that can help both countries improve how children are taught.

I have spent more than 20 years studying education in China and the United States. My passion runs deep for understanding how children and adolescents acquire knowledge and how our schools can enhance the learning process. You might say it is a family calling: My grandmother graduated from New Jersey Normal School for teachers in 1884, my mother was an energetic and creative elementary school teacher, and one of my sisters directed a highly rated preschool. I have taught at most grade levels—from kindergarten through high school—for 14 years, including several years in bilingual English/Spanish primary grades in Pasadena, California. For ten years, I directed the Elementary Education Program at Mount St. Mary's College in Los Angeles. As an educator of teachers, I have spent hundreds of hours coaching trainees in schools throughout the Los Angeles area. Most recently, I developed a program connecting Mount St. Mary's with educators and colleges in China.

My connection with China began unexpectedly as a mid-career graduate student, when I was invited to eastern China to do research for three weeks in the winter of 1990 by my Ph.D. advisor, John Regan, and his colleagues at Nanjing University. John, an expert in cross-cultural communications at Claremont Graduate University, was also a concurrent professor in Nanjing University's English Department for several years. Immersed in helping others understand the complexities and values of different cultures, he provided me and another graduate student the best possible introduction to China. By the end of those three intense weeks in preschools and elementary schools, when I had continuous conversations with Chinese parents, teachers, faculty, and students, my trajectory shifted.

I was hungry to understand what enhances learning and how cultural and language experiences shape that process. I returned to China alone one year later to collect the Chinese part of my dissertation data, and I have returned regularly ever since.

Each trip yields a better understanding of how children are taught in China and, in the process, reveals aspects of American education that I have taken for granted. My research projects, done in collaboration with my Chinese colleagues, have helped peel away the layers of difference in style and method to provide a nuanced awareness of how children learn in both countries. My three-year study of how students in Chinese primary grades learn to write yielded a wealth of unexpected findings about fundamental differences between reading and writing in Chinese and doing the same in English or other languages based on the Latin alphabet. Even the attitude about teachers and education differs markedly in China. In interviews of Chinese parents and students, I learned how, at a very early age, children are taught to show respect for and obedience to their elders at home and in the classroom. But they also spoke of frustrations with an all-pervasive emphasis on exams, adding to my insights about the Chinese classroom environment. Through extensive observations at urban and rural Chinese schools, I've gained the knowledge needed to compare the learning processes in China to those in the United States, which I know so well. I have also engaged in many interviews and discussions about creativity and innovation, and how they are nurtured in both countries, which suggest ways to foster more invigorating school experiences for children in the United States and in China. These are examples of the many paths I have taken to probe the two educational systems, which have provided the impetus and foundation for this book.

Along the way, I discovered that ordinary citizens and policy makers in both countries seem fascinated with aspects of each other's school systems, and some obvious facts emerged immediately. Chinese students score very high on math exams; U.S. students do not. American students are relaxed and talk freely; Chinese students do not. We all know that such generalizations do not apply to all children in a given culture, and we also know that they can lead to stereotypes that do not serve anyone well. Yet, when we compare student learning and teaching practices in the two countries, marked differences stand out.

Americans are intensely curious to know why Chinese students excel and whether adopting some Chinese teaching methods would boost U.S. student achievement. Chinese teachers and parents, meanwhile, admire American students' ability to ask questions and express themselves creatively. This book explores what each country's schools and students do well, and what teachers and parents in both nations covet in the other. The chapters examine the methods of learning and teaching in China and the United States—not to find stark differences or make negative judgments—but to see what we can learn from each other. Finally, the book seeks to define what both systems are missing as our children negotiate increasingly global and competitive twenty-first-century terrain.

Although our histories are dramatically different, both countries have arrived at a strong commitment to publicly financed compulsory education for children—in China for grades one through nine, in the United States for grades one through about ten, when, depending on the state, students can either continue through twelfth grade or drop out. China's commitment to education for all, including girls, began in 1949, with the founding of the People's Republic of China. By 2011, a vast majority of children were enrolled. In the United States, in the mid-1800s, Horace Mann, often called the father of U.S. education, succeeded in convincing Massachusetts to introduce universal education. New York and several other states quickly followed, but it wasn't until 1915 that universal compulsory education had spread to all the states.

The scale of education in the two countries is notable. In 2002—the last year for which comparable numbers are available—the United States had about 54 million elementary and secondary students, while China had more than 200 million, nearly four times as many. There were about 128,000 elementary and secondary schools in the United States versus about 554,000 in China. Within the school systems, though, the structure is surprisingly similar. Children begin with optional preschool years and move on through elementary school, junior and senior high school, and, if desired, to a four-year baccalaureate degree followed by graduate school options. Teacher preparation and credentialing are somewhat similar, although China continues to work hard to bring its teaching force up to higher standards. In the early 1990s, when I began my research, elementary teachers in many parts of China still received their training in what might be called advanced high schools, although high school teachers were often enrolled in four-year college programs. Today an increasing number of elementary teachers in urban areas are credentialed with four-year college degrees, and many rural teachers are able to upgrade their skills and certifications via summer and online courses. Both countries require knowledge of child and adolescent development, methodologies for teaching, and the academic subject areas they will teach. However, unlike U.S. primary school teachers, who are expected to teach many different subjects, Chinese elementary grade teachers specialize in one, and China requires more education of secondary teachers. In addition, U.S. laws allow alternate certification outside of teacher-training programs, but China's do not.[1]

China's education system is governed from the top down with centralized control held by the Ministry of Education and related departments in Beijing. Chinese mandates for financing, curriculum reform, assessment, and teacher quality all emanate from Beijing. In the 1980s and early 1990s, almost all aspects of schooling were centrally controlled. Before 1986, for instance, all schools in China used the same texts and were often on the same page on a given day. Since then, school oversight has become increasingly decentralized. By 2011, several publishers were given governmental permission to develop varied textbook series, from which education leaders in the provinces and cities could select those that best suit their needs, highlighting a shift toward decentralization.[2]

In the United States, however, curriculum and assessment are controlled by state and local governments; there is a complex interplay between states and the federal government. Although national legislation regulates some areas of teaching—for example, requiring strategies to aid low-performing students and those with special needs—states control such areas of their school systems as curriculum content and teacher certification. University of Pennsylvania professor Richard Ingersoll, who conducted a six-nation comparative study of teacher education, found the U.S. system to be unusually decentralized.[3] A concern over low achievement scores, when compared with other nations, prompted a trend toward greater national oversight. In 2002, Congress passed the No Child Left Behind (NCLB) Act, an attempt to improve education for all American children. It imposed annual mandates that have forced schools to focus teaching on passing tests of reading, writing, and math, while deemphasizing or dropping other subjects. After nearly ten years, a backlash from parents and teachers—as well as school districts that face a loss of federal funding for not improving test scores sufficiently—has led to calls to give states more independence. Meanwhile, in 2011, what are called "common core standards," being finalized by a task force of state school officers and others with a stake in education, were gaining traction throughout the country; however, each state is free to adopt them or not.

Curiously, as the debate has raged over how to improve U.S. student test scores during my years of research in China, I've witnessed a fundamental irony. U.S. educators seek to emulate the Chinese by producing more academically focused students who score higher on international exams. But Chinese educators, for more than a decade, have been trying to reduce their reliance on exams that dominate their curriculum and their students' lives. The Chinese seek the spontaneous, innovative, student-centered elements of the American curriculum, the very things being diminished in U.S. classrooms as we adopt more and more of the standardized testing that the Chinese find so suffocating.

Since that morning at the zoo when Feng and I unearthed the mismatch in our parenting views, the same discrepancy—parent-directed learning versus minimally directed exploration—has emerged in my studies and the studies of many others of learning in China, from preschool through high school. In a revealing investigation of how middle-class U.S. and Chinese parents help their four-year-olds use a new toy, researchers found that they approached the task from remark-ably different perspectives. The study, led by Xiao-lei Wang, a professor of education at Pace University in New York who grew up in China and attended Nanjing Normal University, reported that Chinese mothers actively took charge of their children's engagement with the toy, asking them to pay attention and giving them guidance.[4] The mothers demon-strated how to operate the toy and gave additional instructions, making sure the child understood. Next the child was asked to perform part of the task and explain what he or she had learned. The parent immedi-ately corrected any mistake the child made. American mothers, on the other hand, asked their child questions about how to proceed or how the toy operated. They occasionally proposed alternatives, but gener-ally provided guidance only when the child had tried different methods and failed.

When the researchers divided the mothers' responses into three categories—mother-directed, child-sensitive, and child-directed—the difference in U.S. and Chinese approaches became even clearer. The Chinese mothers directed their children's interactions 87 percent of the time, while the American mothers did so 7 percent of the time.

My first reaction to these findings, as a Western parent and teacher, was that Chinese mothers left nothing to chance, nothing for their children to discover on their own. Where was the excitement, the spon-taneity? I think of early childhood years as a delicious time to develop learning capacity by exploring and asking questions, as well as a time to be introduced to new experiences and information. It is a time for children to be excited about new knowledge, to find some things out for themselves, and to gain a feeling of accomplishment in doing so.

From my Western perspective, the Chinese way appeared to deaden the learning environment. The Chinese child was instructed well, but only rarely allowed to explore, to make mistakes and learn from them. That was my instinctive, ethnocentric reaction, based on what I have learned to value as a parent and an educator living in the United States. I am sure this belief has been passed down from my parents and grandparents and generally absorbed from the cultural habits of people around me as I grew up. Most Chinese parents, I suspect, would view my perspective as lax and not purposeful enough. Feng certainly did. I also know, from years of experience studying education in China, that Chinese parents love to have their children experience new things and explore, but in different ways than I am used to.

My current Chinese research colleague, Yu Zhenyou, is critical of many Chinese educational practices but he also believes that we in the United States miss many opportunities to strengthen children's learn-ing, starting in preschool. Here lies a paradox of what we envy in each other's educational system. Americans want students to study harder and learn what they are taught with more seriousness, but we give them considerable latitude to use trial and error to discover the answers, believing that will help develop their thought processes. We teach them to make connections between their lives and ideas and with the material they are learning, without emphasizing the need for intense study of the material at hand. The Chinese want their children to have better ways to explore ideas and to think in open-ended ways, but they are inclined to carefully instruct them on what they should be learning and how they should learn it, therefore keeping them from thinking more expansively and in new ways. Basic learning patterns in both countries appear to reinforce and strengthen the very traits we want to change or eliminate.

In follow-up interviews with the mothers in the study of preschoolers and toys, Wang and her colleagues asked why they interacted with their children in the way they did. The Chinese mother's typical response was, "Young children do not have the ability to finish a task on their own. Adults should direct them and show them so that they know how to do it next time." The common explanation from American mothers of the preschoolers was, "Children can explore and learn on their own. Our role is to guide them, but not do things for them."[5]

Harold Stevenson, a University of Michigan psychologist who carried out decades of comparative studies in the United States, China, and Japan, observed that Chinese mothers said repeatedly that their children's primary task once they begin school is to do well in their studies. "The mothers' own job is to try to do everything possible to ensure that success," Stevenson wrote. "They regarded education as critical for their children's future."[6] U.S. parents, by contrast, generally viewed childhood as a time for many different types of accomplishment, in addition to doing well in school. It is a time to learn independence, to become an integral part of the family, and to take on household responsibilities. It is also a time for non-school activities—music lessons, Girl Scouts, church, baseball, youth soccer, and learning how to ride a bike and swim. Parents view these activities as providing enjoyment as well as opportunities to develop physical and mental abilities, learn social skills such as cooperation, and possibly develop long-term interests. Chinese children, too, take many types of lessons—piano, calligraphy, gymnastics, and chess—and participate in other activities, such as school performances for special occasions or writing short articles for the children's pages of local online newspapers. But in China, these activities tend to be more formal and academic, directed toward specific outcomes and certificates of accomplishments. Such things as intramural sports leagues are beyond the experience of most Chinese families, who place more value on organized educational pursuits than do families in the United States.

The two countries' different perspectives on learning ability are even more fundamental. Americans tend to give more credit to natural ability, making such comments as, "She's very good at math; that's why she did well on the exam," or, "He is so lucky because he has a natural ability to learn languages." I have said similar things about my children and their friends—even as an explanation of my shortcomings. Americans may value hard work, especially in earning a living and supporting a family, but there is an underlying belief that natural ability and native intelligence play a major role in school achievement. The Chinese, in contrast, value dogged effort and believe that anyone can succeed by practice and working harder.

One friend, An Wei, who grew up in a poor village in Shaanxi Province in the middle of China, was the first in his village to attend high school and college. Among many other accomplishments, he has become an interpreter for presidents and diplomats. An Wei, like most Chinese, believes that hard work helped him overcome his limited abilities. In one interview about his college years, he told me,

> As a student you must be good. You have to be the top student. But I'm a slow student. I'm not clever or smart enough compared with many of my fellow students. I had to spend more time studying than the others because I'm not a quick learner. In high school, I spent most of every Sunday studying, but in those days we could not stay up very late because at 10 p.m. the whole school turned off its lights. So I always got up at least one hour earlier than the other students and did my morning reading and memorizing and reading aloud before they got up. That's how I became a good student.

This reminded me of the opening sentence of Confucius's *Analects* (I.1): "Is it not pleasant to learn with constant perseverance and application?"[7] This sixth-century-BCE scholar studied long and hard the work of earlier philosophers and wise men. His disciples recorded Confucius saying, "I wasn't born with innate knowledge. By learning from the ancients, I sought it through diligence."[8]

The writings of Confucius have been interpreted and reinterpreted by scholars and leaders in China and elsewhere across the millennia, but his basic message has been consistent. Differences in ability do not matter; developing one's potential is what counts, and that requires work.

The Confucian tradition is obvious in modern China. Students bend over their books for many more hours each day than do children in the United States. Although some U.S. parents and educators lament heavy homework loads—and some schools do pile on plenty—it is nothing compared to what is expected of children in China.

Jin Li, a researcher at Brown University, and her colleagues have studied differing cultural attitudes about achievement.[9] They, too, found that in the West individuals tended to attribute academic success to ability, while Chinese students attributed success to effort. But she also documented that, to a lesser degree, Americans recognize that effort counts and Chinese students acknowledge that ability plays a role.

Stevenson, the University of Michigan psychologist, in his seminal research comparing learning perceptions and outcomes in China, the United States, and Japan, found that "Americans are much more likely to point to the limitations imposed by an assumed level of innate ability." When he and his researchers asked children in China and the United States to rate the importance of various factors for doing well in school, Beijing children "emphasized effort rather than ability," while Chicago children thought both were nearly equal in importance.[10]

In part this has to do with what teachers emphasize to their students. An Ran, at the University of Reading in England, discovered that Chinese parents in England for graduate studies clashed with their children's British teachers.[11] Not unlike the American mothers of preschoolers, the British teachers viewed children's skills as developing gradually and they were tolerant of errors. The Chinese parents, on the other hand, were paying attention to accuracy. When a child did not get a perfect score, the parents felt it was their responsibility to find out how their children could improve. They also were frustrated that the British teachers spent more time praising the children than pointing out their weak points.

The British teachers, Ran found, thought emphasizing children's achievements would build confidence and spur them to learn more and to advance academically. The Chinese parents could not understand this perspective.

In researching studies about perceptions of hard work, I found a 1990s essay by a Chinese scholar aimed at helping Westerners understand Chinese education. Su Shijun,[12] from Hubei Medical University, emphasized the diligence required of Chinese students and included two rhymes he said could be seen on the wall of Chinese homes:

The only way to cross the mountain of books
lies in diligence;
The boundless ocean of learning requires
persistence in rowing.

The second was the words of a song:

> I am a small boy, a small boy,
> going to school with a satchel on my back.
> I fear not a burning sun,
> I fear not a lightening storm,
> But I fear that the teacher will say that I am lazy;
> Without learning, I have no face to see my parents.

Wondering if they were obsolete, I sent both rhymes to a number of acquaintances in China to see if they were familiar and if, indeed, their children are exhorted to use them. They responded instantly, assuring me everyone in China knew these rhymes and that they could send me many more "working hard" sayings.

One mother said her kindergarten-age daughter loves to sing about the boy with the satchel, a poem written by a Tang Dynasty poet over a thousand years ago. "Everybody in our country is familiar with it. It has been set to a beautiful melody and is very popular among Chinese young kids." A mother with a child in fourth grade said they used these and many more, including: "A young man who doesn't work hard will spend his old age crying," and "Time and patience could grind an iron rod into a pin."

This doesn't mean that diligence comes easily to Chinese children. One parent, Liu Jiantao, with a son in junior high school wrote:

> I think these sayings are correct and I am persistently using them to teach my son the importance of working hard, but it seems that they do not work as well with him as they did with me. My son seems to find little fun in working hard, compared with how I felt when I was young. He finds the Internet and computer games more satisfying than achieving something at school, and so far he is not worried about the future at all! When we were young, we didn't have so much fun outside the classroom, so we were rather keen on "climbing the mountain of books" and "crossing the ocean of knowledge."

Brown University scholar Jin Li and her colleagues have found that these fundamentally different views about how knowledge is acquired— through hard work or with the aide of ability—lead to different ways of teaching and attitudes toward learning.[13] In a complex set of studies, they asked several hundred students at elite American and Chinese universities to list as many learning-related ideas as they could and found that there was almost no conceptual overlap between the choices cited by the two groups.

The American students focused on what the researchers called a "mind orientation," while the Chinese students revealed a "virtue orientation." The Americans saw knowledge as a neutral body to be acquired, and they distinguished between this knowledge and an individual's traits that make it possible to learn, for example, a person's inclination to challenge or question.[14] An overwhelming 96 percent of the American students talked in terms of facts, information, skills, and an understanding of the world. They acquired these through such traits as cognitive abilities and intelligence on the one hand, and by thinking, communicating, and actively engaging on the other.

Li also pointed out that while learning was an important part of the American students' lives, it did not seem to be "intimately connected to their emotional, spiritual, or moral lives."[15] In contrast, 79 percent of the Chinese college students defined knowledge as "a need to self-perfect" and "spiritual wealth/power." They viewed it as "indispensable to their personal lives."[16] For them, knowledge included not only the external body of information that Americans talked about, but also social and moral learning. They valued external knowledge for its usefulness, but did not view it as the ultimate goal. "For Chinese students, the purposes of learning are mainly to perfect themselves morally and socially, to achieve mastery of the material, and to contribute to society," the study concluded. "To accomplish these aims, the learner needs to develop the virtues of resolve, diligence, endurance of hardship, perseverance, and concentration."[17] These virtues are viewed as enduring personal behaviors that can be applied to all learning activities and processes. In a separate study, the Brown University researchers found these same differences of perspective in American and Chinese children as young as four years old.[18]

Li's findings highlight essential differences in how our two cultures approach and view learning. They also provide a glimpse into the complex differences that characterize learning and schooling in China and the United States. I am reminded of an experience described by Peta McAuley, a psychologist who had lived a long time in Hong Kong. In the 1980s, her children, raised by Western norms, attended one of the city's first experimental bilingual, bicultural schools, where half the classes were taught in English by Western teachers, the other half in Chinese by Chinese teachers. When she and her husband attended a conference to learn about their children's progress, the Western teacher described them as "bright, enthusiastic, with strongly enquiring minds." The well-regarded Chinese teacher, however, said their children were "disruptive, distracted, and always interrupting the class with questions." There could not be a clearer example of the difference in expectations—in behavior as well as modes of learning.

My research, reinforced by that of others, shows that societies, in general, cannot take an idea from another and successfully transport it into their own when there is no cultural foundation for it. American and Chinese education systems are at the core of our cultures, and we can only change them by thoughtfully and carefully introducing new ideas. Some, admittedly, are more easily transferred than others. A structural change (for instance, giving U.S. teachers more hours to collaborate as Chinese teachers enjoy) can be instituted fairly easily, as long as the money is found; having teachers and administrators use those hours for substantive collaboration and improving each others' teaching practices is another thing altogether. Decreasing China's reliance on the all-consuming college entrance exam may be a laudable goal; but replacing it with an equitable path to enter college is a far more difficult challenge, one that cannot just be copied from another country.

Parents and teachers in each country continuously ask me how and what they can learn from their counterparts. In China, they ask how to develop more spontaneity in their students, to get them to be more innovative and interactive. In the United States, they beg me to find out how Chinese students learn to pay attention in class and develop strong study skills. How, American parents and teachers want to know, can they teach their children and students to be more diligent?

I don't believe that one system is good, the other bad. It is not my intent to create a furor as author Amy Chua did with her book *Tiger Mom*.[19] In both the United States and China, I have heard almost universal criticism of her harsh tactics for rearing and teaching children. Rather, I appreciate the realities and nuances of American and Chinese schooling.

I have learned that both Chinese and American educational systems have great strengths as well as needs for improvement if their societies hope to meet the challenges of our digitized, globalized world. In the following chapters, you will see the patterns of learning each country engages in, and usually takes for granted, and examine how each does things differently. In order to learn from each other, we need to dig deeper into the methods and attitudes of our respective school systems. We should not try to copy each other's habits; they may not grow in unfamiliar soil. But we can, and must, learn and adapt techniques that are useful for educating our young giants, the leaders and innovators of the twenty-first century.

2

The Teacher's Role

Catching my breath after a hair-raising ride through the crowded rush-hour bicycle traffic, I watched an energetic demonstration of math and Chinese lessons from the back of a school auditorium in the Chinese industrial city of Xuzhou. I had been invited to study this new curriculum that was being introduced at the city's best school. Afterward, my interpreter, Gong, and I walked the halls, video camera rolling, to the headmaster's office for tea and a briefing about the school's aims. Xuzhou, where major rail lines intersect, lies 400 miles south of Beijing, and I was the first Western teacher to visit schools there. It was March 1991. The lessons I saw were similar to what I see today.

The next afternoon, after watching children stream from the school—the younger ones skipping and running to parents and grand-parents, the older students chattering in groups or hopping onto bicycles—Gong and I joined 15 teachers in a staff meeting room. Gathered around a large table, our hands wrapped around ceramic cups of steaming tea to ward off the late winter chill, we began an energetic exchange. It was my first formal meeting with elementary school teachers in China.

We had plenty in common. We were concerned about our students' progress. We wanted to give them the best learning opportunities possible. We shared the belief that to do so we needed smaller classes and constant improvement of our skills. But as we talked, qualitative differences began to emerge. Where U.S. teachers want classes to be kept to 30 students or less, the Xuzhou teachers hoped for fewer than the usual 60. Their school day was much longer, ending at 4 or 5 P.M., but they had a two-hour break when children went home for lunch. Their school year was about a month longer than ours.

They asked me to describe the responsibilities of their U.S. counterparts. As I described what U.S. elementary school teachers do, a few began murmuring to each other. They seemed confused, and the teacher whose class I'd observed the previous day asked me to explain again.

"An American elementary school teacher remains with the same class all day and is responsible for teaching all subjects," I repeated. "We teach reading, writing, math, social science, science, health, art, and music. The children are with the same teacher all day."

Again, they looked at each other and several more began murmuring among themselves. The head teacher sitting beside me added hot water to my cup and attempted to clarify what I had said:

"You teach all subjects then? All of them?"

"Yes," I said, equally puzzled by their confusion. "At my school we are fortunate to have an art or music specialist to give a lesson every few months. That is a great treat, but in general, we teach everything."

It dawned on me for the first time that these Xuzhou elementary teachers did not teach all subjects to one class. I asked what they taught.

"I teach Chinese to the lower grades—what I think you call reading and writing," said one.

"I teach math," said another.

"I'm the art teacher."

"I teach Chinese to the upper grades and I am the director of class activities."

And so it went around the table, specialist after specialist describing their duties. Some taught two subjects—such as social science and calligraphy. But most had only one.

"You teach those all day?" I asked. "How many periods?"

"We teach three or four classes a day, depending on our other responsibilities," explained the head teacher, a woman with short black hair and a print scarf that brightened her somber brown suit.

Stunned, I asked her, "What do you do the rest of the day?"

"We plan with each other, work with students having difficulty, and grade papers," she said, and went on to describe lengthy discussions about how to help students comprehend difficult concepts. They sometimes spent hours planning a single lesson or developing questions to ask their students that would help the children understand a challenging point.

Their experience was so far removed from mine that I found it hard to imagine. The conversation sparked hundreds more questions in my mind. I wondered about the differences between the teaching environments of our countries' schools, the ramifications for students, and, most of all, what we could learn from each other that might work in our respective cultures.

Back in my room in a humble teachers' college hostel that night, I wrapped myself in one of the three woolen blankets the maids had piled on my bed and settled into an armchair to expand on the day's notes. Through a window in the unheated room, I could see snow drifting down. It was mid-March but the heating system in the concrete building was always turned off March 1, no matter what the weather. Boiling water was plentiful, though. I laced the hot water with rum and wrote, trying to capture every morsel of the afternoon discussion and compare their teaching arrangements with those in the United States.

I had taught English in high school for a few years—six periods of classes, one free period for preparation—and every night I lugged home stacks of papers from 150 students. A 30-minute lunch period was usually uninterrupted. When I began teaching in elementary schools, life altered dramatically. My 30–35 students produced papers that were much simpler to correct, but there were virtually no breaks in the school day. From the first morning bell—and often before it rang—until the last student left campus, there was no respite. Finding time to go to the bathroom was a challenge. The brief morning and afternoon recesses were spent meeting students' needs, running to the office for messages, preparing for the next lesson, or taking playground duty for the 15-minute recess. Lunch breaks were longer, but by the time we shepherded our students to the cafeteria and made sure they were in a line and behaving, there was little time to eat. I learned to gulp lunch in minutes. After school and most nights, I and nearly every other teacher I knew spent several hours planning the best ways to engage students and meet individual children's needs the following day. Teaching was energizing but certainly not easy, and it was vastly different from the experiences described by the Xuzhou teachers.

Over the next 20 years on research trips to different cities, I probed more Chinese teachers about their responsibilities and found that in the urban schools, teachers at all grade levels usually taught only their specialty subject in 40-minute classes a few times a day, and they were not required to carry out the auxiliary tasks of running a classroom. Unlike American teachers, they did not collect tardy notes or absence slips, take children to the cafeteria, or make sure there was enough paper. Others performed those tasks without interfering with instruction time. Between classes, teachers worked at their own desks in large, shared offices and collaborated frequently.

In most rural schools, where resources were more limited and teachers not as well trained, the same basic arrangement prevailed. Teachers sometimes taught more than one subject but they had time to collaborate.

At a typical U.S. elementary school, teachers begin the day on the playground, meeting their students and walking them to the classroom, where they stash backpacks and get out homework folders and other materials they need. Meanwhile, each teacher marks who is present and absent and collects notes such as school fundraiser order forms or papers parents needed to sign. The children recite the Pledge of Allegiance to the flag and school announcements crackle over the classroom loudspeaker. During this settling-down period of about 10–15 minutes, the teacher may give the students a brief assignment—a few sentences for daily language practice or a question to respond to in their journal—to get them focused on schoolwork. If a child comes late, the teacher must return to a computer to mark them present.

Each classroom and school district can be somewhat different. The teacher may start with a lesson for the whole class or have the children begin independent work assignments already written on the board. At other times, the teacher may meet with small groups of six or seven students for 15 minutes at a time, explaining new concepts, going over the work they have done, and encouraging them to talk about the lessons. The rest of the class works independently on the lessons they will later discuss with the teacher when it's their groups' turn to meet. After about two hours, the teacher leads the children to the playground for a mid-morning recess and bathroom break of 10–15 minutes. Around noon, after escorting the students to the cafeteria, the teacher has a short lunch break.

The morning is typically devoted to language arts (what is often called reading instruction) and math. After lunch, teachers usually focus on the other subjects—social science, science, physical education, and health. Most elementary schools have dropped art and music instruction, and, often, other subjects like science, in order to devote more hours to preparing the children for the annual standardized tests in math and language arts.

Throughout the day in most U.S. elementary schools, teaching is interrupted by phone calls and loudspeaker announcements asking for a student to come to the office, a group to go for a vision test, and for other varied purposes. An aide or leadership team member may stop by to ask the teacher a question. When I ask U.S. elementary school teachers if instructional time is ever interrupted, the usual exasperated response is, "All the time." They are frustrated that precious teaching time is lost when they have to refocus their students' attention, especially the younger ones, after each interruption. Some schools prohibit such distractions during instructional time, but that is rare.

In China, students are assigned to the same class for the duration of their school years and the teachers of the various subjects go to the classroom. Although schools and provinces vary in their routines, most students begin the day with a half hour of self-study. Students hand in their homework and those who have assigned chores, like erasing the board, do them. Soon they settle down to read aloud Chinese and English lessons, math formulas, and sometimes the Confucian *Analects*.

The *banzhuren*—the teacher who directs a particular class as it progresses through the grades—is responsible for taking attendance and contacting the parents of absentees and latecomers for an explanation. The *banzhuren*, a teaching position that does not exist in U.S. schools, is paid more and works longer hours, overseeing all the extraneous paper work and behavior issues of one class. *Banzhuren* set up class rules, handle conflicts among classmates, and make sure the morning physical exercises—usually led by students—are performed well. They also report regularly to the headmaster about the class and complete end-of-semester reports for each student. "They take care of everything," one parent told me. "Classroom attendance, classroom performances, group activities, sports meets, student fights, classroom hygiene, field trips, lunch at school, just everything. Usually they receive pay. And it is considered an honor to be a *banzhuren*, because of the huge responsibilities."

After the self-study period, regular classes begin. Throughout China, the subject teachers wait outside the classroom door until the students are in their seats with their textbooks out. They then stride in purposefully, saying, "Class has now begun!" The student leader tells everyone to stand. They rise and say good morning to the teacher, who responds, "Good morning, class. Please sit down." The lesson begins instantly, and not a second is wasted for the next 40 minutes.

There are no interruptions. If a kitchen worker delivers food for lunch later (students often eat in the classrooms), it is done unobtrusively. Chinese teachers control the class in a more formal way than do U.S. teachers. They ask for individuals or the whole class to respond to questions about the text. When individual students respond, they stand to give their answer and sit down only when the teacher tells them to. When teachers introduce new material, students respond to rapid-fire teacher questions. Although Chinese government reforms have introduced the concept of working in small groups, few schools use them in any meaningful way.

No independent work is completed during classes and no discussions with the teacher occur. Independent work is done at home and if help is needed teachers sometimes give it during their free periods.

The children have snack and bathroom breaks of 5–10 minutes between each 40-minute lesson, and at some point in the morning, they take a longer recess for morning exercises on the playground. Children move unsupervised in and out of the classroom during the recess breaks, some heading to the bathroom, some playing outside the classroom, and others doing their homework without a teacher present.

U.S. and Chinese schools are more alike at the junior and senior high levels—classes are longer with subjects taught by different teachers. Two points of difference are that the Chinese school day is longer and Chinese students are assigned to a group for the three or four years they attend the school. The teachers come to their classroom, and when the students go to computer lab or gym, the class goes together.

The most striking difference between the two education systems is the nature of professional development for teachers. In China, it is built into every school day and is continuously integrated into lessons at all levels—elementary, junior high school, and senior high school. In the United States, however, it is primarily left to the individual and is voluntary and haphazard. Yet another difference is that Chinese teachers are part of a collaborative community: They share an office, often with colleagues who teach the same subject. As a result, they regularly confer about lessons, their students' needs, and about how to help them.[1,2] In contrast, the American teacher generally operates alone.

Wang Xingye, a Chinese history teacher from Guangzhou who spent a semester observing high schools in Los Angeles, was struck by the fact that American teachers work in isolation. "In China, teaching history is team work rather than individual work," he wrote in his final report on his experiences. "Chinese teachers always prepare their lessons together." Wang teaches at a "key" school, one of many pilot schools across China where government curriculum reforms are first tested. Key schools get more resources, and parents vie to get their children admitted to such schools in hopes of bettering their children's college entrance test scores.[3] But at all Chinese schools, experienced and new teachers work together to ensure that all students benefit from quality curriculum and instruction. They also observe each other in the classroom and discuss each other's teaching methods. "They believe that academic excellence comes from collective lesson planning and team-teaching activities," Wang wrote. "So, the teaching . . . is more unified and standardized."[4]

In contrast, American history teachers "prepare their lessons individually," Wang observed, with "few conferences among teachers in and beyond their schools." He said that although they have much more freedom than Chinese teachers to choose curricular content and instructional procedures, they seldom benefit from structured collaboration.

All Chinese schools have *jiaoyanzu,* teaching research groups within each school. They observe each other's classes regularly and share critiques and research. In 2009, on a visit to an enterprising school in a poor village in Shaanxi Province, in the center of China, I joined several teachers and a few members of the village's education committee at the back of the classrooms. It was one of their regular visits to observe how lessons are taught and later give feedback to the class instructor. It was not the first time I had seen this. At another school, I met a team of teachers who had traveled from a nearby county to observe and comment on lessons. This is the norm in China, and it is done in the spirit of cooperation, not disapproval. Teachers only occasionally visit other schools, but they regularly watch and later critique their colleagues. Equally important is the time set aside weekly to plan lessons together and analyze what their students do not understand and why they don't grasp it. By working in collaborative teams, these teachers continually improve their own teaching skills.[5,6]

In U.S. schools, collaboration only happens in rare situations when two or three teachers discuss their teaching because they see value in doing it—and they do it on their own time. I worked with an innovative teacher who taught in a classroom next door to mine to develop shared projects for our first-grade students, including an exploratory science unit that culminated in a morning at a nature preserve and an afternoon of related investigations at a park. When she moved to another school district a few years later, we met occasionally on Saturdays to explore and brainstorm ideas. We were exhilarated by the learning process and the prospect of finding new ways to engage our students. Many teachers I know also attend workshops on weekends or during summer vacations to learn new techniques and explore how to use innovative teaching materials. They figure out independently how to bring what they learn to their classrooms. Chinese teachers do seek some extracurricular training, but it is combined with their in-class observations and teamwork in an ongoing process.

Administrators in a number of U.S. school districts understand that collaboration could help their teachers. A few large districts have tried to develop ongoing peer-observation programs, using regular teachers and mentor teachers who usually have no classroom responsibilities of their own. However, because substitutes had to be hired to replace the regular teachers, such programs quickly became too costly. U.S. schools do have occasional professional development days, when students are dismissed early or for the entire day. The purpose is often to hold grade-level meetings in elementary schools or subject-specific meetings in high schools, but bureaucratic tasks tend to dominate—such as needing to decide which portions of the curriculum standards correspond to standardized test questions. Sometimes, experts are brought in to instruct a large number of schools about new techniques, such as a new discipline method, or to introduce a new textbook series. Teachers' involvement in their own development is seldom addressed.

The value of bringing in experts for a brief period is questionable. Education researchers James W. Stigler and James Hiebert, who have spent years analyzing math and science teaching videos from around the world, concluded: "Listening to experts during special professional development days does not translate into improved teaching. Effective teacher learning must be built into teachers' daily and weekly schedules. Schools must become the places where teachers, not just students, learn."[7] The experts who talk for an hour or two seldom understand the realities of the classroom. Research evidence shows that supporting teachers with "ongoing, sustained support" improves their teaching and increases student achievement, says Linda Darling-Hammond, an internationally known educator and Stanford University professor.[8] In my own work observing and coaching teachers, I have found that when teachers themselves investigate their practices and how their students are learning, they gain valuable insights about how to improve their teaching.[9] When they do these investigations within graduate school classes or a teacher research group, they are able to get helpful critiques and probe various ways to improve their students' learning.[10]

Wang Xingye, the astute Chinese history teacher from Guangzhou, spent a semester meeting with educators and observing classes in Los Angeles public high schools. As he neared the end of his stay in 2009, we sat on the modest back patio of a Pico-Union neighborhood café near downtown Los Angeles. Mopping up the remaining curried chickpeas on his plate with *naan*, Wang talked about some of the differences that amazed him. Teachers in China should be happy they don't have to work as hard as American high school teachers, he said. "American high school teachers have to teach *five periods* a day. Five periods a day! And they usually teach three different courses within their subject area." After finishing the day, they still have to spend a lot of time preparing their courses and grading student work. In China, teachers prepare only one course and teach it just two periods a day. Wang added, "High school teachers in the United States have no time to plan in-depth subject matter lessons and don't have the advantage of collaborative planning."

The principal of a Beijing high school who was visiting the United States was startled to see teachers assigned to 20 or more classes a week.

His teachers had half that number and used the rest of the school day to discuss and plan effective classroom strategies. "Americans 'teach and teach,' " said Li Jianhua, in a 2007 article for *Education Week*. "They don't have time to communicate with each other."[11]

The observations of Wang and Li Jianhua reflect longstanding issues of concern to U.S. educators. But while we want to see massive improvements as fast as possible and look to China for ideas, my trips across the Pacific have also highlighted positive dynamics in American classrooms worth keeping. U.S. teachers generally encourage students to think and respond without having to memorize volumes of text to be repeated verbatim, as children must in China. Their lessons are much more connected to students' lives and there is less emphasis on high-stakes exams than in Chinese schools. U.S. teachers usually involve all students in discussions so that all are part of the learning process, not just the more vocal, confident few, as is common in China.

In one typical U.S. classroom in an industrial area of Los Angeles, I watched a teacher help 30 fifth-graders match vocabulary words to pictures projected on a PowerPoint slide. Pointing to a drawing of two men yelling at each other, he asked, "What are they doing?"

"Wrestling," said one student.

"Well, I don't think they are actually wrestling, but they are mad at each other aren't they?"

"It looks like they can't agree," said another.

The teacher asked which of their vocabulary words would match the drawing. Some students discussed it among themselves informally, then the teacher motioned to one student.

"They're shouting."

"Yes," the teacher said, "but 'shouting' is not one of the vocabulary words." He paused to let the student figure out the answer.

"Do you want some help?" he asked. "Jose, do you want to help Richard?" Richard and Jose[12] conferred quietly for a minute and Richard tried to pronounce the vocabulary word, 'controversial.' The teacher, who was deliberately giving them time and support to succeed, stepped in to help.

"That's pretty tough to say," he remarked, then pronounced the word slowly for everyone to hear, but especially the many children for whom English is their second or third language. "Now everyone say it—'controversial.' "

The teacher later apologized to me, saying that I'd observed what he called a mundane lesson he thought could be improved. He was especially embarrassed that the picture of two people yelling at each other did not depict "controversial" well. What he didn't realize is that he was giving his students much more opportunity to express themselves, to take risks and openly engage in the learning process. Later, he had also elaborated on the meaning of the word so the students weren't confused. Even inexperienced U.S. teachers give students many opportunities to learn the material at hand, to clarify the lesson with each other informally, and to work in groups or pairs on some projects. They also help individual students think through responses rather than moving to the next student for a better answer.

In another vocabulary lesson, for instance, a relatively new teacher asked a student to contribute a definition, then had others add to it. She also had them turn to their partners and share ideas, using a strategy common in U.S. classrooms known as, "Think. Pair. Share."

"Share with your partner a *superstition* you know."

"Tell your partner when you made a big *mistake.*" The students needed to think about the question individually and then turn to the student next to them and take turns sharing their ideas.

They did it naturally, and it gave all the children a chance to contribute ideas, process the material, and connect it to their lives. Later, the teacher had them form small groups to write paragraphs using the words they'd learned.

Louis Carrillo, an experienced principal at Meyler Elementary School in the Los Angeles school district, would have approved such a teaching method. "To me the mark of a good instructor is giving the kids a chance to produce the answer and practice it in many ways," he told me in a 2011 interview. "You know, when they have a chance to say it five times in different ways and then write it as well, *then* they have a good chance of owning it, of making it their own."[13]

It is customary for American teachers to move around a classroom, from one side to the other, from back to front, drawing closer to a shy student with a soft voice, making sure everyone is on the right page, noticing if someone is having a problem, and drawing everyone into the lesson. Chinese teachers seldom leave the front of the room.

A U.S. elementary school teacher's workday may be grueling, but by being with their students all day, they become familiar with everyone's abilities and needs. During my first year teaching elementary school in a Midwest suburb, I was not able to teach the math lessons because I'd been hired too late in the summer to participate in a workshop for a new math program. Instead, I taught language arts to my class and that of another fourth-grade teacher, and he taught math to both classes. When we met to prepare the first report cards, I discovered the downside of not teaching children all subjects. As we discussed each child's performance, we discovered that some students were excelling in my language arts lessons but were struggling in math and some others, whom the math teacher saw as very capable in math, were struggling in language arts. By teaching one subject to both groups of students, we each honed our ability to convey the material effectively, yet we were missing elements of our students' learning needs, knowledge that might have been helpful in guiding their development. In China, the *banzhuren,* the teachers who follow a class of students through their years at the school, are supposed to gather the information about students across subject areas, yet they tend not to know as much about individual students and their overall progress as most U.S. elementary school teachers do.

Perhaps the greatest difference between U.S. and Chinese education systems is China's near total reliance on high-stakes exams. "Chinese education has only one goal, to get into college by getting high scores on the college entrance exam," educator, author, and parent Yang Dongyan told me when asked to describe the difference between Chinese and U.S. schools. "All schooling in China is aimed at that," she added in a tone suggesting disapproval. They also have to score well on high school entrance exams.

Dongyan and I have had many discussions about our respective education systems on my trips to Nanjing in eastern China over the years. An accomplished educator, she has written books on Middle East policy and taught Chinese to English speakers in China and the United States. She is well versed in the teaching styles and demands of both systems not only because she taught for two years in the United States, but also because her son attended kindergarten and later tenth grade in U.S. schools. In the United States, she said enthusiastically, the system encourages "thinking, doing things, and asking questions." Many Chinese parents and educators I have talked with echo her sentiments.

For more than a decade, Chinese parents, educators, and some government officials have discussed changing their exam-heavy system. A ten-year reform plan instituted in 1999, called the "New Course Standards," mandated more student-centered learning, and more attempts to engage students, out of concern that Chinese colleges were not producing innovators and critical thinkers. In 2010, the government instituted the national guidelines requiring further efforts to engage students and make their learning experiences more interactive over the next ten years.[14,15] But the examination system remains firmly in place. Most Chinese experts agree that the intense pressure to do well on the tests results in an inordinate emphasis on memorization, which effectively undermines most of the reforms.

In truth, although parents and educators complain about the narrowness of the curriculum, everyone in China still expects the same high test scores. The state goals for history teaching are to have students "participate in the teaching process actively" and "develop reflective, creative and critical thinking." But Wang Xingye, the history teacher from Guangzhou, said all of his time is spent preparing students for the national college entrance examination. Moreover, there is also a direct link between Chinese teacher evaluations and their students' scores on the standardized test, which also affect the school's reputation. Therefore, Wang wrote in his final report at the end of his Los Angeles semester, "the teachers push the students harder, while the principals push the teachers even harder."[16] I laughed ruefully when I read this. It is exactly what I hear these days from U.S. teachers who have increasingly been required to prepare their students for government-mandated standardized tests. The words are almost identical.

Putting down her chopsticks at dinner one evening, Dongyan said that after experiencing a year in an American high school, her son grew to hate the Chinese system of education. "The Chinese teachers say, 'Do not ask questions. If you ask why, why, why, you may get confused and then you will fail the exam. Just memorize what I tell you and you will pass.' They say, 'Getting a good score is enough. Too many questions will confuse you.'"

When I asked Liu Jintao, a congenial, soft-spoken parent and English instructor who is also from Nanjing, if she thought this was true, she said the difference between the U.S. and Chinese systems comes down to memorization versus individual expression. "Chinese students memorize everything—in books and even what the teacher is saying." She laughed and added, "Chinese kids have very good memories. They can memorize almost anything."

Each time I return to the United States after studying Chinese teaching methods, I am struck by the paradox: Americans want what the Chinese have; the Chinese want what we have. They crave the individuality and independence found in American schools because they see these traits leading to innovation; we want our students to have the intense focus and discipline that we believe leads to Chinese students' academic excellence. Where Chinese educators and parents say they are desperate to change the iron grip of test preparation, Americans are narrowing the curriculum to increase class time for test preparation aimed at producing Chinese-caliber scores.

Because of the 2002 "No Child Left Behind" Act and its companion 2009 "Race to the Top" legislation, testing has become the focal point in most U.S. classrooms, especially in the elementary grades. Curriculum that creates excitement about learning and thinking is being abandoned as schools devote more hours to practicing for simplistic, multiple-choice or fill-in-the-blank test questions. Teachers are required to give weekly tests to prepare the children for monthly tests designed to prepare them for the yearly tests. Such perpetual teaching to the test leaves little opportunity to foster an enthusiasm for learning among students. In my experience, most American teachers take their jobs seriously and would give their eyeteeth to see their students soar educationally, to develop their full intellectual potential. That has become increasingly difficult to do when the curriculum grows narrower by the month. Some Chinese educators tell me they are astonished that we are trying to reproduce the very testing system they want to abandon, believing it to be detrimental and counter to the education needs of this century.

Despite the increasing emphasis on testing, American students still have many more ways to express themselves creatively than Chinese students do. Dongyan's son was amazed to discover that in his U.S. high school history class, he could select the person he wanted to learn about, do his own research, then write a poem or a play, make a drawing, or give some other presentation to teach classmates what he discovered. He knew he learned far more in this way than by memorizing dry material in his history classes in China.

3

The Confucian Thread

"I'll show you around Confucius's temple," Li Tianchen promised me should I ever visit him at the Qufu Normal University in northeastern China. "Qufu is Confucius's hometown," he added. Li and I had become friends when he translated my dissertation about how young children learn into Chinese. He was a visiting professor at Pasadena Community College near my home in California and his invitation seemed a golden opportunity to explore another corner of China. Although we had spent many hours, with papers spread across an outdoor cafeteria table at the college, discussing the meanings of particular words and, inevitably, Chinese and U.S. education methods, I had barely registered the fact that besides being an English professor he was also the deputy director of the Confucius Cultural Institute. I'd thought that Mao Zedong had eliminated Confucianism from modern China, so the ancient scholar was not high in my list of interests.

In spring 1996, during a research trip, I was able to fit in a side visit to Qufu, 500 kilometers southeast of Beijing. My dissertation defense behind me, I was investigating different types of children's learning in China and the United States. I had spent the first week in Nanjing visiting schools with a research partner, Huang Ren Song. As it happened, we often met by a new statue of Confucius on the Nanjing Normal University campus where she lived. As students paced the edge of a lily pond memorizing dialogues for language classes, we would perch on narrow concrete benches to discuss what we had learned from our classroom visits while Confucius gazed over our heads and children played at his feet.

I had worked with Huang Ren Song for several years, and appreciated her feisty and critical views of Chinese education. My research assistants were always amazed at how modern her research techniques were, even though she began her work in the 1950s when China was emerging from decades of civil upheaval.

"I thought Confucius was in disrepute," I teased one day during a lull in our discussion.

"He's OK now," she said. "Hong Kong donors gave the statue to the college."

I had become used to constant change in China, but the rehabilitation of Confucius surprised me.

Confucianism had been—despite ups and downs of popularity—the foundation of Chinese education and imperial exams for two millennia. Confucian texts were a common body of knowledge throughout the country. When the 1911 revolution led by Sun Yat-sen overthrew the last dynasty, new ideas migrated into China from every corner of the world, especially the West. Confucianism was cast out. The new rulers rejected as anachronisms Confucian worship of ancestors, strict adherence to filial piety, rigidly hierarchical social relationships, and the domination of women by men. Underlying these inflexible social strictures, however, were other philosophical concepts that still remain deeply embedded in Chinese daily life—the belief in aspiring to become a moral person, the importance of hard work, and the need to study in order to improve oneself.

The Chinese Communist Party, which was founded in 1921 and rose to power in 1949, continued the anti-Confucian movement. One of the first acts passed in the new People's Republic of China prohibited arranged marriages, which placed women in servitude to their husbands' family and bound them to the traditional Confucian family system, where females were always beholden to a male. During the Cultural Revolution in the late 1960s and early 1970s, a movement by the party leaders to create a new form of classless society, in which the educated were reeducated by illiterate farmers and most high schools and universities were closed, Confucianism suffered more virulent attacks. But not even the young people who joined the Red Guard could erase Confucius from the national psyche. In fact, the People's Liberation Army protected Confucian family graves in Qufu from being destroyed during the upheavals of the Cultural Revolution.

Eventually, the historical and cultural significance of Confucius was again acknowledged, and as China began to open itself to the world, Confucianism became politically acceptable. Furthermore, the government helped restore prominent buildings associated with the philosopher-scholar and has since established Confucian institutes worldwide.

Toward the end of my time in Nanjing, my friend Lin Jun and I juggled address books, notes, and a flashlight in a dark phone booth to call Li in Qufu and tell him of my travel arrangements.

"I'll be arriving in Qufu at 11 p.m. Thursday night," I said over a hissing phone connection. "And I will need to leave at 10 p.m. Monday."

"You can't stay longer and take earlier trains?" he asked.

There seemed to be no way. Although Qufu lies midway between Shanghai and Beijing on the main north–south rail line, it turned out to be inordinately difficult to get a ticket to there from Nanjing. The university English department chairwoman finally got me one through her sister, who worked for the railway.

In what felt like the dead of night, the train finally pulled into the dark, deserted Qufu station, a far cry from the busy urban centers I was used to. To my relief, Li Tianchen's kindly face looked up from the otherwise empty platform as my train jerked to a halt. Tall and slender with neatly combed gray hair, Li took my suitcase and strode to a waiting car. During the long moonless drive on rural roads to the Qufu Teachers' University, we chatted about inconvenient train schedules as well as the timing and topic for the talk I was to give to his teacher-education students. At the campus hotel, we had to wake the night attendant to get my room key, then Professor Li headed down a dirt road to his home.

In the morning, I watched the people of Qufu hurry along the dusty lanes of the large, semirural campus, carrying thermoses of drinking water and small bags of groceries—perhaps a couple of eggs or a tomato. Parents hustled children along, packs jouncing against their small backs. I wondered if the study habits they were learning had anything to do with Confucius. Li escorted me to his modest first-floor apartment. Entering through the sun-warmed garden in the front yard, his wife greeted me shyly and served up an enormous breakfast beginning with two fried eggs before retreating to a back room.

"She wants to please you," Li said of his wife's breakfast and disappearance. "She can't speak English so this is her way to welcome you." I ate as much as I could manage, not knowing how to turn off the food spigot politely, and soon we were off to tour the campus.

Unlike densely packed urban universities, the Qufu campus had large fields, walkways, and park areas spread in all directions, interrupted by occasional clusters of buildings. Beyond the campus edge, Li pointed to the prosperous-looking liquor factory owned and operated by Confucius's descendants. I found it disorienting to connect a liquor factory with the venerable sage.

At the Confucian Cultural Institute on the campus we headed down broad stairs to the cool basement. "Ancient Confucian texts," he said as we walked into a room of raised, ventilated wooden cabinets with glass doors. "Farmers hid them during the Cultural Revolution." In each sat a small stack of stitch-bound volumes. Their brittle look suggested their age, but I did not know enough about Confucius's writings to ask questions, and I never found out what exactly they were. I assume they were copies of manuscripts of Confucius's teachings passed down through the earliest scholars.

In a large alcove at the end of the room he ran his hand gently along the smooth surface of an old wood table.

"This is where I work," Li said, referring to his personal passion for translating Confucian texts from ancient Chinese to modern Chinese and then to English. It is what he does when he is not teaching English.

"It sometimes takes days or a week to translate a short line," he mused.

The rest of the day streamed by with a talk to a large class of teacher candidates whose limited English probably did not allow them to understand much of what I said, followed by a cheerful English department banquet to welcome me. I had no idea how I would spend the weekend. Li's shy demeanor seemed to keep him from divulging his plans for me, other than instructing me as we left the banquet, "Breakfast at 6:30. We need an early start so we can get to the Confucian Temple when it opens."

Back in my room, unwinding, I pondered a schedule beyond my control. Here was an expert on Confucius offering to spend his weekend showing me what he knew. The tourist guide pages I had with me told a little about Confucius's writings and how they had been central to imperial exams. I realized I might learn more than I had anticipated about the foundations of Chinese education through Li Tianchen's generosity and expertise.

On the way to the temple the next morning, Li and I pedaled on bicycles through wide, dusty streets leading from the campus into the heart of Qufu. Within a half-mile of the temple, I could see new construction mingled with mid-twentieth-century shops. A hotel being built to resemble ancient Chinese architecture, a city administrative building, and a parkway lined with plants were almost completed. Clearly, the municipality was planning to take advantage of Confucius as a tourist draw now that he was back in favor.

Confucius, known as Kongzi in China, lived in poverty and taught in Qufu most of his life (551-479 B.C.E.). A passionate learner and natural teacher, he devoted himself to instructing others on leading virtuous lives that would keep society in balance. Historical records suggest that he craved recognition so that he could test his ideas, but he had little success in his lifetime. For the 500 years surrounding his life persistent social upheavals led to the disintegration of the Zhou Dynasty and vying feudal states dominated. In fact the historical period immediately following Confucius's death is today called the Warring States Period.[1] Confucius held political appointments in the state of Lu, where he was born, for a short time. His idealism and outspoken criticism of rulers' behaviors were unpopular with the powerful since he insisted that they govern for the welfare of society and its people.

Achieving little recognition in his home state, Confucius and his disciples traveled for several years to other feudal states where they were supported by various rulers and attempted to influence politicians. Eventually, political instability and the unwillingness of these rulers to improve their governing led him to return to Qufu, where he taught for the rest of his life. During his last years, he concentrated on compiling major texts from ancient writings, known as the Confucian classics.

After Confucius's death in his seventies, his students continued to spread his teachings and recorded them in the form of brief paragraphs that have become familiar even to many in the West. Each begins, "The Master said."

"The Master said, 'Clever talk and a pretentious manner are seldom found in the Good.' "

"The Master said, 'There are nine things of which Man must be mindful: to see when he looks, to hear when he listens, to be gentle in his looks, to be respectful in his manners, to be faithful in words, to be earnest in service, to inquire when in doubt, to think of consequences when in anger, to think of justice when he sees an advantage.' "[2] (Hardly an attractive philosophy for the powerful men of his day who wanted to steal each other's lands and defeat their armies.)

As I stood at the massive stone gate of the Confucian Temple, Li Tianchen procured tickets at a near-by office and I watched tour groups alight from buses and follow their guides' yellow pennants through the entranceway. Despite its remote location far from major urban centers, thousands of people had flocked to the temple by 9 A.M. Li returned with a shiny gold-colored entrance ticket for me. He chatted with the entrance guard, whom he knew, then we stepped into another era.

The cool of the temple courtyard enveloped us. Engraved stone tributes and monuments rose on either side. We squeezed through a crush of families and factory workers waiting their turn to snap photos of themselves in front of the *bixi*, a statue of a mythical turtle-like creature associated with dragons and long life, into the next courtyard.

At its center was a pavilion built on the spot where Confucius is believed to have instructed his disciples under apricot trees 2,500 years ago. Surrounded by gnarled pines, I stood rooted in place on the courtyard stone slabs, oblivious to the Chinese visitors milling in all directions. I imagined Confucius sitting with his disciples on raised platforms, explaining his teachings on morality and virtue, or walking alone along these very paths deep in thought.

Following his lifetime Confucius's teachings gained in popularity. Over the centuries the temple complex grew into a kilometer-long complex of halls and pavilions that emperors enlarged, renovated, tore down, and reconstructed, adding ever more lavish detail.

As we walked, the tree-lined courtyards juxtaposed against buildings with intricate designs worked their magic, drawing me back in time. I began to sense Confucius's influence as a passionate educator and how his teachings must be rooted in the daily lives of the Chinese visitors who surrounded me.

We sauntered past red-tiled roofs that curved skyward as ceramic, animal-like guardians paraded along their ridges. Looking up at the expansive eaves, Li pointed out the complex of wooden trusses that held up the heavy tiles without iron hardware or bolts.

In the main temple courtyard stood the Hall of Great Achievement, where emperors staged rituals to honor Confucius. I walked past ceremonial drums four-feet across, paused beside a massive pillar, and traced my fingers along the edge of coiled dragon images carved in the white stone. To preserve the sensory feast that overwhelmed me, I snapped photo after photo of carvings, painted eaves, and marble balustrades that underscored the venerated scholar's reach throughout the centuries. Yet I could not help wondering what Confucius, who had lived humbly, would think of these sumptuous surroundings.

We passed scores of other buildings and memorial gates to reach an adjoining mansion where the eldest son of each generation of Confucius's family, the Kong family, resided from the fourth century B.C.E. on, ultimately building it into a labyrinth of more than 400 rooms. Over time, the Kongs became a powerful clan and imperial dynasties allotted them a living allowance in exchange for performing rituals to benefit the emperors. In the mid-twentieth century, however, Mao Zedong's policies drove the official Kong patriarch to Taiwan.

Back on the Qufu campus that afternoon, I wandered among strolling families and wondered how Confucius fit into modern, industrialized China. In contrast to the ancient Western philosophers, like Socrates and Plato, Confucius's descendants still lived in Qufu, more than 2,500 years after his death. An entire volume of the city phone book was devoted to the Kong family; down the road, the Kong family liquor factory turned a handsome profit. On a grassy area of the campus, I visited with two elderly women who were tending their toddler grandchildren and chatted with middle-school students eager to practice their

English on me. How many of them, I wondered, were related to Confucius and, if so, what did that mean to them?

Sunday morning brought another bicycle ride with Li Tianchen— this time heading north, away from the crowds to the Kong Family Forest and Cemetery and the tombs of more than 76 generations of Kong family members, from Confucius to the present. Large trees spread in every direction and I savored the respite they offered from the heat-drenched city streets. We meandered over a bridge and along a walkway crowded with umbrella-shaded vendors selling polished stones they guaranteed would bring goodness into my life, fans adorned with ancient scenes, and Confucian icons. A swarm of Chinese tourists gathered around them, bartering over prices.

A round-faced woman called to Li good-naturedly, "Buy this book, buy this book of Confucian sayings. Your foreign friend will enjoy it." She suggested an exorbitant price for a slim paperback, rendered in ancient Chinese, modern Chinese, and English. They volleyed back and forth over a price. Finally, Li turned the book over, pointed to the author's photo on the back and then to himself. A smile slowly spread across her face as she realized she was trying to sell him a pirated edition of his own book. She bowed slightly and chuckled, touching the tip of her nose in self-deprecation.

We walked on to Confucius's simple gravesite and then biked into the 500-acre cemetery and forest where his descendants are buried. The contrast between the lavish temple and these untrammeled woods of wild grasses and informally placed monuments was remarkable. Few tourists wandered into this vast expanse, affording us a solitude almost impossible to find elsewhere in China as we rode the forest's curving roads.

Granite scholars and imperial officials stood watch, serene and inner-directed, their stone robes etched with the barest of lines. Nestled among the ancient trees were simple yet powerful stone animals. We parked our bicycles, and I walked from statue to statue, the velvet soft grasses of the forest tickling my legs in the dappled sunlight. Li seemed to be enjoying the tranquility, too. As we pedaled farther along the winding road, he pointed out an especially ancient gravestone here and there that dated back millennia. Looping around to the entrance, we rode home in silence, letting the stillness of the woods settle in. It seemed we had touched an essence of China.

The next morning a heavy rain descended. After breakfast with Li and his wife, I returned to my room and watched drenched parents deposit their bundled children into the adjacent elementary school. There had been vague talk of visiting a nursery school, but Professor Li did not seem to have connections to arrange that, so I did not push it. The day was mine to work and explore, but there would be no grandmothers or two-year-olds to share it. The campus community was tucked away in homes, schools, and offices.

I dragged out tape recordings from my research in Nanjing and, with a sigh, began the tedious transcription work. Within an hour my mind had wandered back to the previous days' excursions. How little I knew of Confucius and Confucianism. As rivulets of rain slid down the windowpane, I opened one of two small volumes Li had given me.

"The Master said, 'Only when someone bursts with eagerness of learning do I instruct; only when someone bubbles to speak but fails to express himself do I enlighten. If I show a man one corner of a subject, and he can not by himself deduce the other three, I will not repeat the lesson.' "[3]

This was one demanding teacher, driven, it seemed, by an unquenchable thirst for knowledge. I read on.

"The Master said, 'In any hamlet of ten households, you may be sure of finding someone who is quite as loyal and true as I, but I doubt if you could find anyone who equals my love of learning.' " I flipped pages and read here and there, finding that he continuously emphasized humanity's innate capacity for learning, which he declared was much more important than wealth.

I poured a cup of tea and curled into the worn armchair in my room. Transcriptions could wait. Confucius taught that "instruction recognizes no castes" at a time when only the privileged were given formal schooling. Rich or poor, he chose disciples for only one reason—they exhibited an insatiable desire for knowledge.

How much do his teachings fit with modern schooling in China? Friends often mention Confucius's influence in their daily lives. Robin Wang, an American philosophy professor, brought up in China, described her special attachment to Confucian texts and other ancient writings that shape life in China. They are, Wang wrote, integrated into "the language we speak, the code of conduct we follow, and the living ideal we strive for."[4] Just the week before in Nanjing, two friends had made me a list of important educators. "Whoops," they said, laughing. "We forgot Confucius. He's Number One Educator."

I closed the books and went for a long walk in the rain, returning to pack and join Li and his wife for one last meal. The warmth of our shared experiences lingered as we drove to the station that night. I waved good-bye as the late-night express began to move and watched the station slip away, its lights glimmering in the darkness.

I nodded to two other passengers in my compartment and stashed my briefcase near the head of my bunk. Pulling the window curtain open, I watched the silhouetted countryside glide by as we began the long haul to Shanghai. Thankful that the others had gone to sleep, I mulled over Confucius's influence in the many classrooms I had observed in present-day China and the frequent parent comments about school pressures.

During subsequent trips to China, I took more notice when someone mentioned Confucius. A high school teacher from Shaanxi Province, anxious for me to understand how central Confucius was to Chinese culture, wrote an email saying that Confucian thought has "the most deep influence on the characters of Chinese people." Their hospitality and diligence are derived, he said, from Confucius's ideas. A lackadaisical graduate student from an eastern province, who was more interested in his girlfriend and computers than in studying, lamented that the pervasive Confucian emphasis on learning made him feel pressure to study harder. A friend who is director of a national research institute told me that the Confucian concern for "honoring our parents, of never disgracing them, is in every fabric of society." To fail in school means to shame your family, she said, adding that even those who cannot read follow Confucian principles.

From time to time I have returned to Li Tianchen's translations to better understand how China's history has affected modern school practices.

Both filial piety and *ren,* a word often translated as "benevolence" or "perfect virtue," are fundamental Confucian concepts. A virtuous person must practice courtesy, generosity, and diligence, while filial piety demands that children not only respect, but defer to their parents throughout their life. Confucian teachings hold that relationships are hierarchical, but also that those who are more powerful also have responsibilities to their charges. If a father expects filial piety from his son, he must show a deep love and kindness toward his son. If the son does not wish his father to treat him badly, he must attend to his father with filial piety. Similarly, if a ruler wants his subjects to be loyal, he must have a moral character befitting a ruler. If he does not, his subjects cannot respect him and social stability will vanish. For teacher and student, moral character is still considered an essential element of learning, just as Jin Li found in her studies of Chinese and American college students. The Chinese students viewed knowledge as intimately connected to virtue and perfection of the moral self.[5, 6]

From my perspective, a kindly dictator with rigidly stratified relationships seems to be at the heart of Confucianism. Everyone is expected to behave with respect and kindness. Individuality and striving for uniqueness are not high on the list of prized attributes. People are viewed in relation to how they treat others, not for their independent ideas. Students are expected to maintain respectful relationships by honoring their parents, their grandparents, and their teachers. To do this, they must work very hard. Li Tianchen's translation of *The Analects* and books that describe Confucius are peppered with references to the importance of learning and diligent study. This legacy is evident in the attitudes and work habits of students in today's China, and also in the Chinese curriculum, which emphasizes studying texts rather than learning from experience.

In the conclusion of the Confucian classic *The Doctrine of the Mean* (XX.20–21), reference is made repeatedly to the effort required to become an exemplary person. "While there is anything he has not studied, or while...there is anything he cannot understand, he will not [interrupt] his labour. Let a man proceed in this way, and, though dull, he will surely become intelligent; though weak, he will surely become strong."[7] The pressure to study harder permeates Confucian directives that have been kept alive in China for over two millennia. "The Master said, 'Pursue study as though you could never reach your goal and were afraid of losing the ground already gained.' " Do similar pronouncements govern American education?

Socrates, born shortly after Confucius's death and transmitted to us through his students Plato, Xenophon, and Aristophanes, believed the teacher should guide the student toward the light. His method was to keep asking questions that would move the student toward understanding, not directly, but through reasoning. But rather than following an uninterrupted line to the present, the continuation of Socrates's pedagogy has been tenuous. The Western teaching model has undergone multiple changes. In the eighteenth century Rousseau influenced not only political thought, moving it toward democracy, but also educational thought. He and, later, Maria Montessori valued the natural child but rejected the idea that children were natural reasoners. Horace Mann, who lobbied successfully for universal public education in the early nineteenth century, wanted all children to have the same opportunity for education, so curriculum became more standardized and rote learning was viewed an effective way to give students information.

In the twentieth century, American education seesawed from one belief to another within decades. Dewey introduced the power of experiential learning to schools. This was followed by the views of educational behaviorists who saw children as empty containers that need filling. In rebellion against this notion, classrooms in the 1960s turned toward open-ended, experiential learning to which others reacted and demanded more accountability. The United States lives with multiple educational traditions that appear to positively and negatively influence what is happening in U.S. schools today. Each movement has had a different focus as to the best way to learn, depending upon its goals, and many times acrimony, not compromise, is the result. Although the philosophy of Socrates and his students continues to influence elements of U.S. teaching, with some high schools today using Socratic seminars to enhance students' thinking, no straight line leads from his ideas to the present. Although Chinese history has bent and reinterpreted Confucian teachings over centuries, the trajectory from Confucius is much more direct.

Confucius described himself as a man "whose zeal for work is such that he forgets to eat; whose happiness in his pursuit of knowledge is so great that he forgets his troubles and does not perceive old age stealing upon him."[8] Stories told about his childhood, whether real or imagined, are filled with his single-minded desire to learn, a drive that seems alive and well in twenty-first-century China. In primary classrooms throughout China, children sit up straight, always attentive, responding when called upon, ready to critique each other's renderings of Chinese characters, and answer when the teacher questions. They are diligent and focused. Older students carry these habits forward, compelled by the education system and the need to score high on exams.

Each time I enter a classroom in China I feel an intensity of focus on the lesson that I have yet to experience in a U.S. school. Fast-paced and almost choreographed, not a moment is wasted in a Chinese class. I can almost hear Confucius urging the students to dig deeper to learn, to be more diligent.

4

Depth of Understanding— Mathematics

Xu, a young research partner in China in the 1990s, was anxious as he prepared to take the Graduate Record Exam (GRE), which is required to apply to U.S. graduate schools.

"I'm not very good at math," he told me. "I've always excelled at languages instead."

When I later challenged him to explain his near-perfect math score on the GRE, he said, "But that was very simple math, even for me."

Well, I thought, not for me, and I started out as a math major in college.

Time and again studies and international tests have shown that Chinese children learn math in more depth than their American counterparts. By the time I collected my dissertation data in China in 1991, I was familiar with the research of Harold Stevenson and James Stigler, who had spent years probing the superior achievements of Chinese and Japanese students in mathematics. In a series of studies, they found that Chinese attitudes toward math learning were quite different from those of Americans. They verified the achievement gap between Chinese and U.S. elementary school children and explored possible contributing factors, such as hours attending school, parental attitudes, and the amount of time devoted to homework.

As I spent more time in China, I realized that numerals permeate daily life. From my Western perspective they clutter English descriptions at tourist sites—the size of the site, the number of buildings, and how many years it was inhabited. Magazine articles and website introductions are loaded with numbers. On one university website, the second sentence of a page intended to lure potential students read that the campus covered a total area of 3,100,000 m^2 and had approximately

900,000 m^2 of floor area. I cannot imagine that an American university website would even include that numbing bit of numeric information, let alone in the first paragraph.

Number references also are scattered throughout conversations with my Chinese friends and colleagues. This number is good, that one is bad luck. Americans have a few notable numbers: Show me a tall building with a thirteenth floor or an airport with a Gate 13. But this is nothing compared with the Chinese concentration on numbers. Once while driving along a boulevard in Nanjing with my colleague, Feng, he spotted several wedding couples near a bridal salon where they had rented their attire. Feng pointed to large identical characters pasted on a window behind the brides who were decked in Western-style white or traditional Chinese gowns of deep red.

"Double happiness," he said, smiling at the two characters for happiness on the glass. He enjoyed explaining bits of his culture to me. "Today is September 9. Nine is a very lucky number, and nine-nine means double luck and good fortune. Lots of couples try to get married on this date."

Another time, a friend scooted into a seat at a restaurant table and apologized for being late.

"I was waiting in line to buy this good phone number that didn't cost very much," she explained.

"What?" I asked. "You pay different amounts for different numbers?"

"Oh, yes. The luckiest numbers are very expensive. Some unlucky ones don't cost anything."

"Like what?"

"Like one with fours in it."

I later got one with several fours—it was free. My Chinese friends promised they would call me even though the word for four—*sì*—sounds like the Chinese word for death.

Although my graduate-school research was on how reading and writing develop, whenever possible I also observed Chinese math classes. The first one was a lesson at an elite elementary school in Xuzhou, the industrial city that lies between Nanjing and Beijing. It was to be a demonstration lesson in the auditorium for me, the first Westerner to visit the school.

The 60 or so second-graders took their seats, arranging their pencil boxes and books neatly on a desk-like shelf in front of each row. Without delay, Teacher Ma, a middle-aged woman who had been instructing for several years, held up one flashcard-like slate after another, each with an arithmetic problem written in Arabic numerals. The children sat tall and responded loudly in unison: "$48 + 20 = 68$, $6 + 80 = 86$, $74 + 6 = 80$." They knew addition cold.

I edged forward on my chair, sensing a dynamic I hadn't seen in American elementary school math classes. The children displayed confidence, but also keen attentiveness. Teacher Ma picked up a larger slate and read a new problem, "There are five yellow roses and eight red roses. How many more red roses are there than yellow roses?" She underlined the question with a jagged line as the children repeated it. Gong, my interpreter, translated it for me into English.

The school's assistant director, who was sitting next to me at the back of the auditorium, whispered in English that this was the focus of the day's lesson. I smiled, thinking I had misheard him. Certainly second-graders would not spend 40 minutes on one problem, especially such a simple one. My first-graders had done this kind of problem early in the year.

A drawing on the main chalkboard showed five yellow roses in one line and a row of eight red ones beneath them. Ma then covered the extra three red roses. I glanced at the book of a child seated in front of me. The picture there was somewhat different: There were five yellow roses on top and the eight red roses below them, but this time the first five red ones were shaded out.

On the board:

O O O O O   [5 yellow roses]

O O O O O ▢O O O▢   [8 red roses]

In the book:

O O O O O   [5 yellow roses]

▢O O O O O▢ O O O   [8 red roses]

Leaning over to me with concern, the assistant director explained, in more detail than I could imagine important, that Ma was teaching the concept differently from the picture in the book. First she was showing them that there are equal numbers of red and yellow roses, then she lifted the covering to show the extra three red roses. He said the teachers had studied how the children learn this important concept and decided that the way she was explaining it was better than the book. I was amazed at the minutia of instruction he was describing, but it was obviously significant to him.

Ma had the students read the problem, then turned on an overhead projector, displaying the colored flowers in lines. She covered up the extra three red ones, just like the illustration on the board. She talked about it and had students make observations. My interpreter, who seemed to think all this was commonplace, said they were merely describing the problem in diverse ways. It seemed so simple, yet the children were suggesting many more variants than my students would have.

Opening their pencil boxes, the Chinese second-graders took out homemade counters made from small matchsticks, cut-up plastic straws, and toothpicks with the ends cut off. Each child laid out five in a top row and arranged eight more neatly below them, mirroring the example on the board. My own primary grade students loved to work with physical materials—what are often called "manipulatives" in teacher lingo—but although they tried to create careful patterns, theirs were much more haphazard. These Chinese students were using the materials far more precisely.

Gong leaned over to explain that their task was to determine how many more objects were in the bottom row. I hid my amusement at the ridiculous simplicity of the problem. But the children in front of me touched each of their matchsticks as if counting them. None were sloughing off or goofing around because they already knew the answer as some of my students would have done.

Teacher Ma called on several students to give the answer to the rose problem and explain how they solved it. Then a student was asked to draw another problem on the board—three flags in the top row, eight in the bottom row with five shaded. Still remarkably simplistic.

> > >
> > > > > > > >

The teacher discussed it with the student at the board and others contributed their thoughts. How many are equal? There are three flags on top and three flags on the bottom. Ah, and then there are five more flags on the bottom. That means there are how many more on the bottom?

My impatience grew. They were working with what we call "families of facts." The numerals 3, 5, and 8 are a family—$3 + 5 = 8$; $5 + 3 = 8$; $8 - 3 = 5$; $8 - 5 = 3$. Once my first-graders understood the concept, they loved to do sets of problems with different "families." So why were they spending so much time on this in second grade in a country whose people are known for their mathematical ability?

When the teacher moved to the next problem, I got my answer. "There are 245 girls and 51 more boys than girls. How many boys are in the class?" She projected a diagram that matched the pattern of the earlier two, but with the total quantity for boys missing (see Figure 4.1).

The simplicity of her earlier examples suddenly made sense. The students knew right away that the total number of boys was the number of girls (245) plus 51. The way Teacher Ma had explained the simple problems made this more complicated one easy to think about.

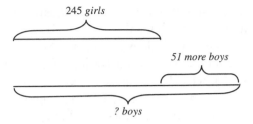

245 *girls*

51 *more boys*

? boys

Figure 4.1   Second-grade math problem, China.

The students turned to their textbook, which this time showed an illustration identical to the overhead slide. They wrote the answer directly in their small paperback books, which they own and which had brief instructional materials plus exercises.

Ma inspected some of the children's work, her relaxed interactions with them suggesting her years of experience. The children checked their answers against the book while one student wrote it on the board. As I watched, it occurred to me that even with my strong interest in math, I would not have known enough about the underlying mathematical concepts to think through the best ways to present the initial problem that would enable students to correctly solve more complex ones.

Teacher Ma put up the next problem—326 red flags, 73 more yellow flags. How many yellow flags were there? As she wrote, she, like other Chinese teachers I had watched, made a coherent visual presentation, writing four problems using colored chalk to highlight similar parts. These differed markedly from the haphazard board notations made by most U.S. teachers in both elementary and high school grades.

As the children completed the flag problem and put away their matchsticks and straws, I made notes about what I had witnessed. Although the type of problems and the manipulative tools were similar to those used in U.S. classrooms, Ma's highly simplified approach to the first problem contrasted significantly. Moreover, her students took these simple problems seriously, and the teacher showed them how to transfer that example to more complicated calculations. Teacher Ma was teaching the children a mathematics lesson; most U.S. elementary teachers merely teach arithmetic.

That night at Xu's home, I pored over the math book of his first-grade son, Xiaowei, and watched the boy complete his homework. He was figuring out lots of problems in his exercise book adding and subtracting two-digit numbers that include a zero—such as $30 + 28$ and $43 - 20$. Interspersed were problems with a single and a double-digit number, like 6 + 15. No page was entirely devoted to the same type of problems, unlike my children's U.S. textbooks.

Xu showed me the lesson Xiaowei had just been taught, problems with one zero. The book used an illustration of beads on a string that focused on groups of tens. The exercise asked the student to add three groups of ten, plus two groups of ten, and then eight individual beads. Xu said that in another month, Xiaowei would begin to carry numbers over from one place to the next. The book also contained beginning multiplication problems, demonstrating the concepts with matchsticks at first. These topics were similar to those I introduced in my first-grade class, but after witnessing the math lesson and seeing Xiaowei at his homework, I now realized that the depth of their learning far surpassed ours.

Shortly after returning to Los Angeles, I read an article by James Stigler and Harold Stevenson titled, "How Asian Teachers Polish Each Lesson to Perfection."[1] Their description perfectly matched the Xuzhou math lesson I witnessed, but they also identified a quality in the lesson that I had seen but couldn't pinpoint. Every aspect of that lesson had been thought through and polished so that the children, over the course of 40 minutes, moved carefully and successfully from very simple concepts to the application of those concepts, and on to much more complicated challenges. The Xuzhou lesson had been a demonstration and as such was undoubtedly practiced. Since then, however, I have seen plenty of unrehearsed lessons and they have also been polished.

Though my research was in a different field, I continued to read more studies by Stevenson and Stigler that took note of specific learning strategies of Chinese students with numbers. California teachers who had Chinese immigrant children in their classes, for instance, noticed that these students were not only good at calculating, but that they also did not like to estimate or round off numbers. They wanted a precise answer.[2]

On subsequent trips to China I watched math lessons that started preschool children on simple algebraic procedures and on comprehending the concept of fractions. I also continued to notice the ubiquity of numbers in Chinese daily life and the ease with which people processed long strings of numbers.

"06390502624," Zhang Li repeated as I wrote her phone number down with appropriate dashes so I could read it easily.

"You don't need to put dashes in," she said, a slight admonishment in her tone. How many times had I heard that comment, that you do not need dashes in a ten-digit phone number? Well, I thought, some of us need to group numbers so we can remember them. And yet, my memory for numbers has increased since I began traveling to China. International calls via phone cards can require up to 52 numbers, and I now usually dial them correctly the first time.

In 2009, I spent a week observing in schools in Nanjing. Having learned many years earlier to avoid the key schools because they receive much more government funding than most others and have a highly selective student population, I had arranged with a friend to observe classes at her daughter's regular school. I followed her along rain-slippery flagstones to a new building where the vice-principal for community affairs greeted us. He showed me around the large, ordinary school buildings, introduced me to the primary-grade teachers who were preparing lessons in their communal office, then to a second-grade classroom. Carrying out an experiment, the school had capped primary grades to about 25 children per class, rather than the usual 50 or 60. However, as in many U.S. schools, small lower-grade classes give way to larger upper elementary and high school classes.

I settled into the back of the room to watch the math teacher for the lower grades enter and the children stand to greet her. The lesson began with not a second lost. With music playing, the students began 40 warm-up problems in their exercise books involving different mathematical concepts. After they finished, one student stood to give the answers.

"33," she said.

"Right," responded all the students.

"10."

"Right."

"183."

"Right."

When they finished, the teacher asked what they had been learning recently.

"Addition of three-digit numbers," said one.

The teacher repeated the answer, and called on another.

"Subtraction of three-digit numbers." No pause came between one activity and the next.

"Good. Today we are going to review subtraction of three-digit numbers."

They turned to a page in their texts with problem sets such as:

$12 - 5$ $15 - 7$
$120 - 50$ $150 - 70$.

"Please find the first question and start doing the exercise. Ready? Go!"

After 20 seconds, she commented that some students had already finished and that the others were too slow. I flinched at such direct criticism, although I had been told more than once by Chinese educators that it was important if children were to succeed. Nevertheless, it bothered me.

Students gave the answers to the problem sets.

"$12 - 5 = 7$," said one.

"Right," they all responded.

"$120 - 50 = 70$."

"Right."

"$15 - 7 = 8$."

"Right."

"$18 - 9 = 9$."

"Right."

"$180 - 90 = 10$."

"Right."

I was amused that the students had not noticed the mistake in the last answer. "Right" had become an automatic response, part of a rhythmic pattern. Well, I thought, the Chinese children may be way ahead of ours in math, but they are still children.

The teacher interrupted quickly. "Ok, now let's have a look at this problem. Is it related to the problem above it?"

"Yes," they replied.

She moved them little by little along a series of steps, getting responses throughout, then calling on a girl in the middle of the room wearing a red jacket, "Good. Gao Xiang, the answer of this problem is?"

"The above problem is $18 - 9 = 9$; this problem should be $180 - 90 = 90$."

"Good." The teacher repeated, "The above problem is $18 - 9 = 9$; the problem below is: eighteen 10s minus nine 10s = how many 10s?"

They all replied, "Nine 10s."

She continued, "Nine 10s =?"

"90," the students called out.

Later, when I had time to peruse the lesson, I was struck not only by the constant speed of her pacing but also by the careful building of concepts and associations. I was sure that most U.S. teachers, myself included, would explain this problem by saying that the students just had to add zeros, whereas the teacher in Nanjing stayed with the basic concept, subtracting tens. Only later did they switch to the short-cut of adding the zero. The Chinese words for numbers above nine helped this concept along, since the numbers 10 through 19 are written "one ten (十)," "one ten one (十一)," "one ten two (十二)," "one ten three (十三)," "one ten four (十四)," and so on. Twenty-five is "two tens five (二十五)," 59 is "five tens nine (五十九)." But even though this idea is built into the language, the teacher still emphasized the fact that these numbers were composed of groups of 10.

Up went another exercise, a table of subtraction problems, each with a minuend (the top part) and subtrahend (the part to be subtracted), with the difference to be calculated. She called on a student near the back who did not have his hand up to describe the rule they needed to use.

"Minuend minus subtrahend equals difference *x*. If we subtract a subtrahend from a minuend, then we get the difference," he responded. The teacher repeated it; then the students said it again in unison. There it was again, the continuous repetition of fundamental concepts. Although this was a very basic mathematical concept, she was making sure the process became automatic, almost a conditioned reflex.

The subtraction problems displayed on a video screen and in their exercise books required borrowing, such as

$$729 \qquad 627$$
$$-439 \qquad -276$$

First the teacher led them through a few questions about the process, then she reminded them that they had to keep borrowing "1" from the larger unit place.

"Can anybody tell us the complete calculation rules?" she asked. "You, Liu Zi Hao, please," she said, motioning to the boy seated in front of me.

He stood. "Adjust each digit place, units to units, tens to tens, etc., and start from the units place." I had never had my students memorize mathematical processes in words. The reason, I decided, was that it would help them only if they thoroughly understood the concepts described. Otherwise it would be useless. But these students seemed to be able to apply this rote learning.

The teacher continued, "If the number in the units place of the minuend is too small to subtract from, then borrow '1' from the tens place and '1' becomes 10." She stepped up on the raised teaching platform. Until then she had been walking back and forth in front of the students' desks.

"Can anybody else tell us the complete calculation rule?" One girl stood and repeated the rule again.

"Very good! Now please use the rules to complete the problems. Ready? Go!"

She gave them 90 seconds to complete five three-digit problems with borrowing. Then, clapping three times to get their attention, she asked if they had any difficulties. She was doing exactly what Liping Ma, the Chinese teacher who had moved to the United States for graduate school, had found in her research.[3] In comparing the math-teaching strategies of American and Chinese elementary school teachers, she discovered that, unlike U.S. teachers, Chinese mathematics teachers continuously encourage their students to discuss the parts of problems they do not understand. Chinese parents tell me, however, that only the bravest ask in class.

I saw a few hands shoot up with no apparent timidity.

"Good," said the teacher, calling on a girl with yellow barrettes in her dark hair. "I see that you, Fan Miao, have a problem. Tell us about it!" The student explained her difficulty, and the teacher walked the children through it very carefully, having different students respond at each step, correcting errors as they went along, and asking students to rethink an answer before moving on to the next portion of the problem.

I know that most American grade-school teachers, who teach five or more subjects, do not have the depth of knowledge to walk children step-by-step through mathematical concepts to prevent misunderstandings. The Chinese math teachers usually teach only the one subject, and in urban elementary schools they specialize in just the primary or upper elementary grades.

The next set of three problems also required borrowing. Three children went to the board to complete them. They needed to write the problems both vertically and horizontally, show all the borrowing, then demonstrate how they checked the answer. The rest of the class did the problems in their books. After four minutes she stopped them.

"Please be quick," she added. Then seeing one child still writing, she said, "You, Wang Hao Ran, stop." She began to clap and the students echoed her. Three claps from the teacher, three claps from the students, five times in a row until the boy stopped.

"Please don't let me clap for so long just because of you," she said to him. Wow, I thought. If I were Wang Hao Ran, I would be paralyzed. Later I asked a Chinese friend with a younger child about it. She laughed.

"He has to learn to be quicker," she said. "Anyone can do it quickly, and if a child needs to work harder than others to accomplish that, well, so be it."

American teachers tend to be much less direct when trying to speed up automatic skill acquisition. Yes, they give plenty of timed tests for math facts—simple addition or subtraction and multiplication tables. But American teachers who expect a lot from students, whether first-graders or high school students, do not approach them in the assertive way Chinese teachers do.

When the Chinese second-graders were learning new math operations, the teacher corrected their errors, helping them see their mistakes. But when it came to the speed of calculations they should know, she was adamant. Again and again during the lesson, she alternated between a rapid-fire response rate required of students when they were doing problems and a studied slowing down as she discussed more difficult calculations.

Liping Ma's in-depth study, which compares U.S. elementary school teachers considered skilled in math with Chinese elementary school teachers at both high-performing and poor-performing schools, found most of the American teachers did not comprehend mathematics in enough depth to catch the mistakes or misconceptions of the students or help them clarify their understanding of a complex mathematics lesson. The Chinese teachers in her study had much less formal education and had taken fewer advanced mathematics courses than the U.S. teachers, yet they had considerably more understanding of the difficulties the students might encounter in mastering elementary school math. More important, they knew how to teach it so that the children succeeded. At least part of this developed from the Chinese teachers' opportunities to study lessons collaboratively and plan how best to present them.

Although Chinese students have an international reputation for mathematical skill, the Ministry of Education has been pushing schools to modernize the curriculum. They see a great need for tying math to real-life situations and moving away from isolated algorithms. New standards were developed in 2001 for grades one through nine and in 2003 for senior high school.[4] Major reforms include a spiral curriculum with the same mathematical areas such as algebra, geometry, and statistics recurring at each grade level. Introduced in first grade they build to more advanced levels in each successive year. In addition, the new standards require the texts to use more learner-centered activities than in the past and the teachers to tie math to everyday life.

For teaching probability and statistics, for instance, the standards emphasize development of a familiarity to deal with problems containing data; an appreciation for the role statistics plays in decision making by using data collection, graphic displays, and analysis; and an ability to read data resources and summaries critically. In grades one through three all children are expected

> . . . to be able to compare, arrange and sort objects according to some criterion; have some experiences of collecting, recording, describing, and analyzing of data; learn to use pictograms, bar graphs and tables to display data and use the mean to summarize a group of data; learn to obtain information from the media (newspapers, magazines and television programs); explain ideas to other students based on data; identify deterministic phenomena and [chance] phenomena; list possible outcomes of simple experiments; understand that different events can happen with different chances and be able to describe chances qualitatively.[5]

In fourth through sixth grade they should be able to do these at more advanced levels; design simple questionnaires; and understand and use mean, medium, and mode appropriately. They should also learn to read statistical tables and graphs in the news media and understand that they can be misleading, learn the concept of equal probability and fairness of a game, be able to calculate probabilities in simple situations, and design a game to let an outcome based on chance happen.

For the very early grades, Li Jun, a math reformer at East China Normal University in Shanghai, suggests the following type of activity to learn about "average" or the "arithmetic mean."

> Five girls and five boys each have some pencils.
> The number of pencils are:
> Girls: 3, 3, 6, 3, 5
> Boys: 2, 2, 6, 2, 3.
> Do the girls have more pencils than the boys? Explain your reason.[6]

The students should not just calculate the answer, but describe how and why they arrived at it. They should also be encouraged, just as the students in the Xuzhou second-grade lesson I observed, to think of as many different ways to solve the problem as possible. Using their responses, the teachers should then move them toward more complex statistical understanding.

For statistics in high school, students might be asked to study the height of a group of people. They would first collect data for everyone in their class. Then each student would select a random sample, figure out the sample mean, and compare the different means they found. They would then calculate the mean of all the samples trying out different formulas to discover the most effective.

Li Jun, who works on mathematics reform within China and internationally, has found that although some teachers have adapted to the new curriculum standards, many find them difficult. In a 2004 survey, 90 percent of those teachers questioned said they continued to use a lot of older material, and of junior high school students queried, about 75 percent said at least half of their homework was comprised of exercises not in their new textbooks but required by their teachers. Li says that in reality students enjoy doing learner-centered activities, but teachers are not willing to use them because the college entrance exams do not measure the type of learning that results from them.[7]

My observations of classes throughout this reform decade that began in 2001 have suggested that, as in the United States, major change requires many years to take effect. Although in all elementary grades I have seen the use of more student-friendly textbooks, an increased informality of teaching styles, and introduction of group work, fundamental curriculum reform is slow to emerge. In high schools, except for a few special ones, it is seldom evident.

The familiarity with numbers in Chinese culture cannot be exported to the United States, nor can all of the in-depth, everyday use of mathematical knowledge accrued over centuries, but we can ask what would happen if our elementary teachers did not have to teach five or more subjects. We can also ask how we could improve mathematics instruction by giving teachers time to study together the typical difficulties elementary children and high school students have in grasping basic concepts and to work collaboratively on explanations that could give their students a deeper understanding of mathematical functions.

5

Pressure and Exams

L in Jun, a feisty English language professor, and I sat at a side table in one of Nanjing University's restaurants while wedding merrymakers celebrated nearby. We often spent mealtimes discussing new ideas for teaching English or one of her books on applied linguistics, but tonight she was preoccupied with her granddaughter.

"Chun-Chun would enjoy this," Lin Jun said, a lilt at the edges of her matter-of-fact tone as she motioned to the wedding party. "But you know, she has to spend all her time studying so she can get into a good high school. She cannot afford to take time to have dinner with us. The entrance exams are only a month away."

I found it hard to fathom the pressure China's students lived with. Chun-Chun was 11 years old, and it was Friday night, with no formal school the next day. (Saturday school attendance had been eliminated several years before.)

I was sure that my high school-age son and junior college-age daughter back home in Los Angeles would not be spending their Friday evening studying, no matter what was due the next week. I liked their ability to push serious study aside and play, even though I have gotten angry when I felt they were sliding through an assignment. The rigor and pressure of the Chinese educational system seemed oppressive to me.

I asked Jun how her spirited granddaughter was doing. Since the child had entered primary school, she had been a challenge, I recalled. She was very independent—like her grandmother, I surmised. One memorable day, Chun-Chun had gotten angry with the teacher and headed for home.

"She's okay," Jun said, "but she hates this studying. Her mother has to keep after her all the time." Jun picked up the menu to order, then added, "You know, she'd do much better in an American school where she could have a little more freedom, more chance to move around. Chinese schools aren't made for children like her."

I was in China for a month of language study in the fall of 2003, and when I was not untangling Chinese sentence structure and memorizing characters, I jotted down stories about people's experiences. Many involved exams and school pressures. My research partner, Zhang Feng, talked about the "little yearly exams" his preschool daughter had to pass to enter a good primary school. A host in Xi'an, in Shaanxi Province in central China, told me that his son was studying nonstop for the national college entrance exam. He had taken a year off after high school to prepare for it full-time. It sounded as though the 19-year-old boy was under house arrest.

In another friend's home, where I spent a lot of time in 1991, I had watched his first-grade son complete two hours of homework each night. Even on the boy's sixth birthday, he and his friend had to read lesson passages six times and write the new characters of the day until they knew them by heart. Next they began their math assignments. Only when they had finished and demonstrated their proficiency could the party begin with long noodles representing a long life.

"If they don't begin to study like this now," Xu Jian-yuan said, "they'll never get into college. There are two thousand years of pressure to do well in school in China." He laughed, but I knew he was deadly serious.

In 1991, Chinese higher education institutions had slots for just 5 percent of the senior high school graduates who were applying to college, and the only path to admission was a top score on the college entrance exam. It is this knowledge that led Xu, his wife, and other parents to lament how difficult it is to crack down on their children when they enter first grade. Unlike the casual atmosphere of preschool, the children now needed to sit tall and pay attention all day, learn the discipline and precision required to write Chinese characters, then complete hours of homework.

One of the most difficult ideas for Westerners to grasp is that the Chinese college entrance exam score is the sole basis for university entrance. There are no references, no student essays, and no extracurricular activities or grade-point averages to boost their chances. Students' educational futures and, to a great extent, their professional opportunities are determined by one number, achieved on a two-day test. The Chinese say it is "like thousands of troops on a single-log bridge" because of the limited number of college spaces.[1] This single score determines not only the university they will attend, but also their academic major. In China, students are accepted to a specific department within an institution, not to the college or university as a whole.

High school students in the United States also are under pressure to score high on national academic tests, but they can increase their chances of being accepted to a college or university in multiple other ways. References, grade-point averages, school-club responsibilities, special projects, volunteer work, and more can enhance their credentials. Even though U.S. students may find juggling their academic load and extracurricular activities stressful, the combination of experience allows them to demonstrate their abilities—academically, in leadership, and in originality. One typical undergraduate I interviewed, for instance, had formed an organization to raise money for orphans while in high school. He also got an internship with a project that gave him substantive work experience. Because his test scores were not as high as many others, he was sure that these other activities had given him the edge he needed to be accepted to his college of choice. If U.S. universities and colleges used only a single test score for acceptance, parents would be up in arms. This would also deny admission officers the information they need to create a student body that is balanced in academic interests and leadership abilities.

Many in China condemn the reliance on one exam; others defend it. Critics see it constricting education to a curriculum of test material, which forces students to devote their lives to memorizing for the exam. Defenders point to the fact that it is unbiased and provides the only means for the poor and those without societal know-how, such as college-educated relatives or connections to influential people, to gain university access. This is especially true for students from rural areas.

An Wei, the first from his poor village to finish high school and college, and who returned to improve education there, passionately defends the exam system, saying that if it broke down, graft would be the only way students could get into college. History suggests that while the current system is hardly perfect, it is fairer than anything else that has been tried. During parts of the twentieth century, for instance, Chinese colleges used personal references, which became a means for the children of corrupt officials to gain admission.

In fact, the exam and the resultant pressures it produces are a way of life in China, entangled with centuries of historical and cultural habits. For most of the last 2,000 years, nationwide imperial exams were held to identify talented candidates from all strata of society for governmental posts. Although the system favored those who were well off and had access to tutors or clan schools, they were a means to broad representation, and Confucius is central to this practice.[2,3]

Indeed, Confucius's ideas might not have persisted for two millennia were it not for the imperial exams. One of his major goals was to find solutions to the governmental chaos of his time. He turned to ancient texts that predated him by several hundred years and devoted enormous energy selecting parts of them that he thought would help citizens and rulers. The books he compiled became known as the Confucian classics. After his death, the first ruler of all China, Qin Shi Huangdi (221-207 B.C.E.), tried unsuccessfully to burn all the books to prevent Confucian ideas from spreading. By the first century B.C.E., however, Confucian teachings regained popularity, and Emperor Wu Di decreed Confucianism the official state philosophy, creating five institutes aligned with the surviving Confucian classics—*The Book of Songs, The Book of History, The Book of Rites, The Book of Changes,* and the *Spring and Autumn Annals.* Wu Di also decreed that government officials be chosen on merit, as defined by exam, rather than by wealth or powerful connections, as had been the tradition. From then on, for most of the next two millennia, the Confucian classics formed the basis of school curriculum and the content of the imperial civil service exams.[4,5] The more I have read about this history, the more difficult it is to fathom. Nearly 2,000 years of an exam based on the same five books? I cannot imagine what it would be like for the state of California to retain the same fundamental knowledge base for even 20 years.

As literacy spread throughout the centuries, more and more people took these exams, including individuals of humble means. Men (women were not allowed) often began studying classical Chinese at age six and continued daily drills and memorization through their twenties or thirties, or even longer, until they were ready to tackle the exam. Families made great sacrifices to allow one of their own to devote himself to such studies, and a man who failed the exam could disgrace his relatives as well as himself.

What's more, some Chinese families began their children's memorization process before age five. In fact, Confucian texts were the first primers used to teach young children to read.[6] No wonder Confucius's teachings are pervasive in modern China. Whether Confucius himself recommended memorization is unclear. To a Westerner, the technique seems antithetical to Confucius's inquisitive mind. However, from the earliest times, reading texts aloud multiple times has long been a Chinese method for unearthing their meaning.[7] Chinese scholars down through the ages memorized Confucian classics, which have, as a result, become deeply embedded in Chinese culture.

In 1905, the imperial exams were abandoned, as they were viewed as irrelevant to modern needs. But the college entrance exam was introduced in the early 1950s when the newly formed People's Republic of China began the reform of national testing policies.[8] Universal education did not exist in China at the beginning of the twentieth century, and although several modern universities had been established, they served only a small number of privileged students. With the birth of the People's Republic of China in 1949, public elementary schools and then secondary schools were introduced throughout the country. Then, during the Cultural Revolution, high schools and universities were shuttered for 11 years and elementary schools were turned into political forums. One early glimmer of hope at the end of that devastating period was the opening of universities by Deng Xiaoping in 1977. Space was limited for the droves of education-starved young people, competition was fierce, and admission was gained by means of an entrance exam. Topics for the entrance exams were related to elementary and high school curriculums. Fierce competition continues today and, as in past centuries, failure translates into dishonor for one's family.

By the early 1990s, when very few slots existed for college aspirants, China began a massive effort to increase the number and size of universities to accommodate more students.[9,10,11] To finance and streamline growth, the government introduced one change after another. Entrepreneurial trends had made significant inroads into China by then, and universities were required to help support this expansion by starting commercial enterprises. Nanjing Normal University, for instance, which specialized in the education of quality teachers, went into the lamp business, tore down a building fronting a busy street and opened a shop. They sold home education workbooks on the side.

Such innovations did not continue for long, but some colleges were successful and used this impetus to leverage industrial funding. One university acquired a substantial number of computers and launched night and weekend courses for businesspeople, an enterprise that has prospered and led to other profitable activities. The commercial phase was followed by a consolidation period, with university leaders overseeing massive mergers that combined general academic institutions with aeronautical institutes, medical universities, and more. This too faded away as colleges hunted for more feasible ways to increase their student capacity.

Meanwhile a few private institutions struggled to emerge, an innovation accompanied by heated controversy in this centrally governed country.[12] I was privy to the beginnings of one, Xi'an Translators University, and I greatly admired the grit and tenacity of its founder, even though he viewed higher education as a money-making scheme, reasoning that "customers pay before they receive a product."[13] By 2011, though private colleges still were not accredited to grant regular degrees, students could take an exam to acquire a government-issued bachelor of arts certificate.

In recent years, public universities have established large private colleges attached to them as an income source. Tuition is considerably higher than for their parent institutions and their degrees are less prestigious. However, this trend has expanded the number of slots for China's vast student population. In 2008, about 300 such colleges existed, but the government has slowed their development because of the lack of quality controls.[14] Many do provide students with a substantive four-year college education, but according to a professor who is part of a college evaluation team, there are others that give students the equivalent of a two-year community college education in the United States.

The Chinese college entrance exam, the *gaokao*, is administered throughout China once a year for two days in June. Traffic is limited around test centers, loud construction is halted, and parents are held at bay as more than 10 million students bend over their papers.[15]

The exam includes three mandatory subjects—Chinese, mathematics, and a foreign language—and three others. In most provinces the students must select their college major before they take the exam. Although requirements differ somewhat by province, science majors have to take the standard subjects of physics, chemistry, and biology. For those majoring in the humanities, history, geography, and political studies are tested. In the early 1990s, I was told that exams were uniform across the country. Since then, however, provinces have been given greater latitude in how to organize the exams.[16]

Administered in regular school classrooms, each sub-test includes an objective section answered on a machine-scorable paper and an open-ended portion—such as an essay in the Chinese language subtest—that is graded by teachers after it has been scanned into a computer with all identifying marks removed.

Parents and grandparents wait outside throughout the exams. Said one Beijing student I interviewed, "My parents were just outside the building, and they were more nervous than I was." A student from Sichuan, in western China, said his parents waited both days, then nearly a month to learn his score. Others said their parents accompanied them to the exam hall, but then went home to wait.

U.S. college applicants suffer through the Scholastic Aptitude Test (SAT) or the ACT[17] exams, put together by competing organizations. There is no national, governmental exam, and in fact, not all colleges require an exam. If students opt for the SAT, they take a general test that includes sections for writing, critical reading, and math. The writing and math portions have open-ended responses as well as an objective section. To increase their scores, and presumably their eligibility, students can also take up to three subject matter exams of their choosing, such as biology, English, or a language. If they get an undesirably low score, they can retake any part of the exam. Almost all of the exams are offered every two or three months. In China, when students fail, they can retake the exam, but not until the following June.

In the United States, test preparation courses are available, as are online programs and myriad books with sample questions. For those aiming at the most selective institutions, the pressure can be intense. However, SAT or ACT scores are only one part of an application package and students have many other ways to distinguish themselves, including a personal essay and interview. But, their Chinese peers live in a far more pressurized world. Those who have attended key schools—the most prestigious schools, primarily in the wealthy eastern provinces—arrive at the college entrance exam with enormous advantages. The same can be said for American students who have been privileged with prestigious private school experience, but the gap in China seems to be wider. Rural schools are far shorter of materials than poor U.S. schools and frequently lack qualified teachers. I was in one rural school where the fifth-grade Chinese teacher barely knew how to write his name.

In the United States, although high school courses do not ignore the looming SATs and the subsidiary state exams, the school day is not dominated by them. In China, all three years of senior high school are aimed toward the one exam, and the entire curriculum, beginning much earlier, consists of test preparation, primarily through memorization. This is true of all schools and even for students who are not planning to attend college.[18] The process starts with tests at the end of preschool to gain entrance to the most sought-after elementary schools. Tests at the end of first grade give access to the best second grades within a school, and so on.

In 2004, I helped rural high school teachers practice oral English during their vacation. Two other Westerners and I, with our enthusiastic "let's loosen up and learn" point of view, tried to engage them in impromptu dialogues, pretend phone conversations, and any games we could think of to help them relax and use comprehensible English. They were polite but resistant. Although the Chinese organizers of the project wanted to provide these rural teachers with their first opportunity to talk with native English speakers, the teachers wanted only to memorize vocabulary and have us explain fine grammatical points. Perhaps this was partly a way to avoid facing their fear of talking with us and exposing their poor oral skills, but they also sidestepped our efforts because none of our activities would help them teach their students. They told us over and over that they had no time for such informal activities in their classes. They had to stay exactly on track with the nationally developed textbook lessons day after day, and their students needed to memorize every word if they were to pass the college entrance exams. We did succeed in getting them to talk more freely, and by the end of three weeks, most appreciated our approach, but they still viewed time devoted to comprehending and using oral English a luxury.

Later, one of these teachers emailed me as he was preparing his students for exams:

> We are engaged nearly 12 hours a day and seven days a week in teaching our students, who have only about 50 days left to prepare themselves for the college entrance exams in early June... You can never fully understand how terrible the teaching situation is in China![19]

When I wrote back agreeing that I did not understand the exam pressure they experienced, he responded:

> The exams in China are really awful, sometimes too much for both students and teachers! That may be the reason many people in China can't be as creative as they are supposed to... Can you imagine that my students have to take practice exams every evening, from 7:30 to 10 for two weeks before the real exam, and at weekends they have to take more formal practice exams? What's even worse, my son, Daniel, in grade three has to do such things at school and at home.[20]

Students have corroborated this many times over. Those who attended rural high schools, where boarding is common because of the long distances, said they were not allowed to go home on weekends for the last three months before the exam, nor could family members visit. One girl told me the only benefit from exam preparation was that "we girls lost weight."

A student from Sichuan province in western China who, much to his relief, had made it to a well-regarded eastern university said that several months before the exam, many students in his high school class felt depressed.

Some in government and a slowly growing group of psychologists are concerned about the effect of such intensive study and the push by parents to excel. But because competition is so fierce for so few spots, and traditions so entrenched, little has changed. Hope had been high when a new minister of education was appointed in 2009, but parents say as far as they can tell, nothing has changed.

In 2007, while I was sitting in the Nanjing airport lunch area with Liu Liang and his wife waiting for my plane to Xi'an, our conversation turned to the exams. They said many students develop serious psychological problems because of them. Liu Liang, now a successful businessman who travels the world, said he grew up in a poor rural family, and by the time he began first grade, he was used to hours of manual labor. Learning about urban life from magazines, he studied endlessly to pass the college entrance exam and escape his grueling farmwork. During senior high school, he never slept more than five hours a night in order to memorize enough for the exam. He passed, but was a wreck. Now, 15 years later, every time the national exam for high school seniors approaches, a nightmare returns: The teacher places the exam paper before him, he looks at it, his mind goes blank, and terror engulfs him.

Liu Liang and his wife believe the high-pressure life of most Chinese urban kids is debilitating. They make sure their junior high school-age son completes his hours of homework thoroughly at night and on weekends, but unlike other Chinese parents, they do not pack his extra time with cram sessions, piano lessons, and other activities to enhance his competitiveness. They describe him as an average student, but a happy child, unlike many who are excelling.

Throughout China, family life is governed by exams, beginning in the primary grades and increasing in intensity as students move through the grades, reaching a fevered pitch in the last year of high school. When Yu Zhenyou, my current research partner, picked me up at the Beijing airport one year, I commented on the pillows stacked in the back seat of his car.

"They're for my son," he said. "He needs to have as much time to relax as possible while he's studying for exams because he's in his final year of high school. With the pillows it's easier for him to sleep while we take him to school."

Although their son had studied diligently throughout his school career, their family life was held hostage to his studying. "Every minute of our lives is aimed at helping him succeed," Yu said. "It is essential. This is the Chinese student's life."

Aspirations and competition are high, and students set themselves nearly impossible goals for university entrance. Gao Qian, a friend in Nanjing, reported that even the last year of junior high school is filled with extra weekend and evening classes just to earn a high score on the high school entrance exams. Most of the 14- and 15-year-old students begin studying for this the year before, the equivalent of eighth grade in America. The better the high school they get into, the thinking goes, the better opportunity they will have to score high on the *gaokao* and gain admission to a prestigious college. Gao said parents are run ragged trying to help their child prepare.

Even teachers compete with each other. Gao said his fifth-grade son described one teacher who had come to his math class while it was in session to announce that three of her students had gotten into an elite high school. Such high scores were unusual for his son's school, Gao said, adding, "The only reason she did this was to brag and make the other teacher feel bad in front of her students. This, in turn, pressures the other teachers to pressure the children."

In his report at the end of a semester as visiting scholar for the Los Angeles-Guangzhou Sister City Association in 2009, Wang Xingye, a Guangzhou history teacher, said although over half of high school graduates are able to attend some sort of college, the fierce competition to gain admission to the prestigious universities is debilitating. Educational administrations, from the national to the school level, adopt detailed measures to improve student scores, and the school, the local school district, and the provincial education department all develop tests that mimic the national exam.

There is a direct link between student test scores, a teacher's evaluation, and a school's reputation. To win promotions, principals push teachers harder, who in turn increase the pressure on students to get good exam scores.

In the United States, while some students feel pressure to get into the eight Ivy League schools and a few other prestigious universities, many more are interested in a large variety of other colleges and know that they'll get a valuable education that can lead to reasonable careers. In China, on the other hand, educated parents direct their children to the 10 or 15 "top" universities in the country. When I ask why a second-tier college would not do, I'm almost always met with the same anxiety-ridden response: A second-tier college will not offer a good path to a job that will provide their child with an adequate living. In 2010, there were an estimated three million unemployed or underemployed college graduates in China.[21]

Yu Xi, a young professor who was a visiting scholar at my U.S. college, described an ongoing debate among parents about whether a student should get a good degree from a less famous university rather than an overenrolled major, such as English, at a prestigious one. She said saving face usually wins, and the parents and the student select the famous university that offers an unemployable major "because the student and parents can say, 'I'm in so-and-so university.'"

This need to "save face" in Eastern societies is difficult for Western-ers to fathom. In the United States, "to lose face" might be described as embarrassment or chagrin at not having succeeded, or possibly as shame. But saving face in China is an ever-present, compelling force that shapes many life decisions. It may even undermine the Chinese government's efforts to make education more student centered and engaging, as parents pressure teachers to increase academic prepara-tion for the exams. The result: a narrow curriculum that is trapped in memorization.

"Schooling is all memorization," said one professor, "from first grade on." One reason the children can respond to teachers' rapid-fire ques-tions in elementary and high school classes is that they have memorized the texts and know they must pay attention every minute of a lesson if they are to perform well. An American high school teacher teach-ing English in Xi'an told me with amazement that her Chinese middle school students could remember classroom dialogues from weeks ear-lier. At her Pittsburgh school, she said she was pleased if her students had read the current lesson.

The Chinese parents who say they would prefer that their children have more open and creative schooling concede that it is not possi-ble. One parent, Zhou Dandan, who had a son in the last year of preschool, summed it up this way: "In all the elementary schools, the atmosphere is strict. If your child is somewhat different, then he will have trouble adjusting to the situation. So you have to teach your child how to behave so he is prepared to take exams in the primary grades."[22]

One solution that middle-class and wealthy Chinese parents have found is to have their children travel to other countries for their under-graduate education and avoid the *gaokao*. They study only for the exams required of overseas universities and colleges, such as the Test of English as a Foreign Language (TOEFL) and the SAT. Some prestigious Chinese universities now are offering a one- or two-year course to help stu-dents pass these tests, and businesses have formed to help them apply to Western universities, mostly in the United States or Australia. The number of Chinese undergraduates in the United States has increased dramatically. Before 2007 it was about 9,000 annually. In the fall of that year it jumped to 16,000, and according to the Institute of Inter-national Education, it had risen to 130,000 in 2010, a huge rise from 2007.[23, 24]

As standardized tests gain the upper hand in American education, schools—especially elementary schools—are forfeiting projects that encourage independent and collaborative thinking, discussion, field trips, the arts, and substantive study of a variety of subjects that could enhance children's reading and math abilities. They are being replaced by mind-numbing drills and test practice. It would be wise to learn from China's disillusionment with exam-driven schooling.

6

The Influence of Language

"Please read the new word and the phrase, Li Jia," Teacher Wang said, motioning to a girl in her second-grade classroom.

The Chinese language arts teacher walked back and forth on a raised platform in front of the room, scanning her young students. They sat tall on backless benches at wooden desks. Qiu Wei, my research assistant, and I watched from small chairs tucked in behind the children. It was 1996. We were at the Nanjing elementary school that Qiu Wei had attended 20 years before.

The girl stood to speak. "*Sheng, sheng. Anhuisheng, anhuisheng.*" They were learning to read a passage in their textbook about a famous mountain in Anhui Province, and the new characters to learn included *sheng* (province) and *anhuisheng* (Anhui Province).

"She pronounces quite well," the teacher told the group.

"You, please," Wang said, pointing to another child.

"*Sheng, sheng. Anhuisheng, anhuisheng,*" the student read in a strong voice.

"*Sheng, sheng. Anhuisheng, anhuisheng,*" the class repeated.

The rhythm accelerated, the energy high.

"Which province are we in?"

Fifty-five students answered in unison, "Jiangsu Province." On they went, probing the text about a beautiful place in southern China and pronouncing new words as the teacher referred to posters of Anhui Province mountains taped to the blackboard that matched pictures in the students' textbooks.

Choreographed precision and intense focus. Precision and focus. So unlike the flexibility and informality of American classrooms, I wrote in my notes.

"Why is Yellow Mountain famous?"

Students raised their hands. "Sun Na, you tell us," Wang said.

"Hot springs, special rocks, pine trees, and eh . . . ."

The teacher interrupted and directed her to sit down. "You'd better give a complete answer. And your voice is too low. Who would like to answer more loudly?"

More students raised their hands. "Chen Chao, please." Chen Chao stood and responded.

How humiliating for the girl, I thought. As a Western elementary school teacher, I have always strived to create a positive learning atmosphere. Teacher Wang's criticism made me uneasy. I was used to correcting students more indirectly to build their confidence as they learn.

Leaning over to Qiu Wei, I asked, "Doesn't that bother the students?"

"It's not a problem," she said. "This type of exercise is very important so they can speak and read well."

At the end of the intense instructional period, Qiu Wei and I walked down the hall to a first-grade classroom for another language arts lesson. This one about Mingming, a curious boy who is tempted to chase a cricket in the weeds, but is persuaded to stop such mischief by a friend so he won't be late to school. The teacher probed the first-graders the same way as the second-grade teacher, mixing together detailed interpretation of what is happening in the story with a focus on new characters that are being introduced. Half way into the 40-minute lesson, the teacher stopped the class for a three-minute song break and shifted to studying how to write Chinese characters, beginning with a rhyme all schoolchildren must memorize:

The body is one fist's length from the table.
The eyes are 0.3 meters from the paper.
The fingers are 0.03 meters from the tip of the pencil.
Good eyesight is important to us all.

Even their rhymes emphasize precision and focus, I thought.

The children traced the new characters in their paperback textbooks while the teacher drew three moderate-sized squares on the board. She selected students to write one of the day's characters in each square, urging them to strive for balance and accuracy. The others compared their peers' attempts to book examples.

Pointing to one square, the teacher continued, "Now let's look at the character, *zhui* [追] that Zhao Yu wrote. Is it good or not? Tang Jia."

Tang Jia stood and said in a clear voice, "This character is not good."

"Why not good?"

"Because this character should be in the shape of a square, but it is rectangular."

The teacher picked up a piece of red chalk. "All right. Look. This stroke of hers is quite good, but that stroke is not so good and it should be written like this." She corrected it.

"Right? The two parts are too close." She wrote another line on top of the student's attempt. "So now this character looks like a square. This stroke should be in the center of the square. Zhao Yu, next time you write this character, please pay attention to these places."

For 20 minutes, the class continued inspecting and correcting details of the characters and identifying differences between similar ones. I could not imagine U.S. elementary students staying focused on such detail or accepting criticism so easily.

The recess bell rang. The students stashed their book in the desks and grabbed another for the next class. Qiu Wei and I thanked the teacher and headed for the director's office as children streamed outside for recess. Chinese jump ropes were pulled taut and ping-pong balls zipped across small concrete tables. Hopping and skipping students whirled around us, just as children do on a U.S. playground.

Back in my dimly lit hotel room that night, I mulled over the lesson we'd watched. At home in St. Louis, Missouri, and then Pasadena, California, I had taught most elementary grades, and had spent considerable energy investigating how children developed language, especially written language.

I kept returning to China because I was intrigued by how Chinese children's learning was affected by a world with a written language so totally different from that in the West and by an educational system that had used similar teaching strategies for millennia. What struck me about Chinese schools was the focus, even with the youngest children, on detail, accuracy, and fast-paced repetition. This was particularly noticeable when they were studying Chinese characters that are the building blocks of their language.

I tried to envision my first-grade classroom an ocean away in Pasadena. Everything worked so differently there, and I suspected the reasons had a lot to do with the very structure of our two languages.

I could imagine feisty Danielle bent over a paper, her seven-year-old fingers clutching a thick blue pencil and mouthing the sound of each letter she drew. "Sssss, ssss, ssss. Uh, uh, uh. En, Ennnnn."

Then she would straighten up and admire her large, unsteady letters. "Sssssuuunnn. Sun," she read, and would lean forward to begin the next word. The concentration we ask of the children in our U.S. classes is so unlike what was demanded of the Chinese children I had watched that day. We teach our students phonetic rules and devote only a little time teaching them to form letters; Chinese students are taught how to form each stroke and the components of each character in detail, but little time is spent on the very vague phonetic hints contained within the characters.

I encouraged my first-graders to write independently, using word lists in the room, but also to invent their own spellings when they did not know the correct one. I smiled thinking of some of their attempts. At the beginning of one school year, Kimberly, bouncing with enthusiasm about her sister's piano recital, wrote, "We went to a residol. Ter wur a lot uv pepol. Sum plad the pano, sum dedet. They sat down. The End." Kimberly had huddled in a corner of our crowded classroom, focused on her task like a professional writer. Inventiveness took over when she did not know conventional spellings. Letter sounds took the place of more complex vowel structures such as the "a" in "plad" (played), and she spelled some words the way they actually sound, like "uv" (of), "wur" (were), and "sum" (some). As the year went on, she learned more about how the letter system works and became a fluent, young writer. Her confidence grew during the months because she was encouraged to express her ideas in writing by blending skills learned in class with her own spelling inventions.

My 30-plus students sat at clusters of desks and worked by themselves part of the time. My aide and I taught reading lessons in small groups, allowing the others to complete follow-up work independently. When they finished what was required, we encouraged them to read something from the classroom library, to use activities on bookshelves that reinforced reading and writing skills, and to write freely. Their independence was possible because they learned to sound out words and use other strategies to unlock pronunciation by themselves. Chinese characters are just not like that.

I often began instructional lessons by having my students read words aloud. At the beginning of first grade they are simple ones: *cat, mat, sun, had, am, the, they, all, in, see, me, tree.* When they stumbled, as some do, on *tree,* I pointed to each letter and they made the appropriate sound, then blended them together. There was no need to focus on the details of forming the letters. They seldom confused them.

Just before this trip in 1996, I had taught a demonstration lesson for a beginning teacher about the *ent* family, words that end with *ent.* This helps reinforce sounds the children have learned, and shows them how patterns in words can enhance their ability to recognize them quickly and read fluently.

"*Eh, en, te,*" the children said as I pointed to the letters.

They blended them together, "*ent.*"

"What ends in *ent*?" I asked.

"*Went,*" said Rocio.

"*Spent,*" said another. I wrote as they dictated.

"*Tent.*"

I added one, *rent.*

"*Bent,*" said Stephanie.

"*Cent,*" said Jose, adding, "It's money." He smiled shyly.

"How do you spell that one?" I asked.

"S-e-n-t," said Jose. They hadn't yet learned that the letter "c" can be "hard" or "soft." I did not correct him directly. He was just gaining confidence as a reader. I wrote *sent* and *cent* on the flash cards I was making, added "1¢" after *cent* so they would know which was which, and put them in a cardholder for their future use. I assigned them to find other *ent* words for extra homework, then began a lesson on sentence structure.

I placed an eraser under an overturned box lid, then asked where it was.

"Under the lid," Jose said. He was definitely gaining confidence.

"You're right."

I put my hand under the table. "Where is my hand?"

"It's under the table," Roxanne said.

"Where is the pencil?" They pointed to the pencils in the jar beside the table.

"Tell me."

Manual raised his hand. "The pencil is in the jar."

I made sure each child had answered a question, then took out a strip of poster board with the question "*Where is the _____?*" Their assignment for the next period when they would be working independently at a table, I explained, was to complete the question with different items. If they wanted to, I said they could also try to answer their own questions.

How different this open-ended lesson is from the Chinese classroom, where the whole class is focused on repetition and precise details. I signaled my students to stand and push in their chairs. The children rotated in groups to the next set of clustered desks. It took a few minutes for them to gather materials, but when I motioned to get busy, they settled into the next lesson.

A teacher from China, Gao Qian, who observed classes in a Los Angeles elementary school could not get over how different they were compared to his fifth-grade son's class in China. He was astonished.

"Your students have time to relax and think," he said. "Beginning in first grade, my son and all Chinese children have to focus for every single minute of a 40-minute lesson. Every minute. The energy our children pour into this is incredible. They cannot let their minds wander. At night they study every detail of the characters and their textbook lessons, memorizing them all so they are prepared to answer the teachers' rapid-fire questions." He spoke passionately, frustrated by the pressure his son felt.

The languages, themselves, seem to control our teaching styles. U.S. first-graders have to learn the 26 letters of the alphabet and the multiple sounds they make. But once they know quite a few of them, they can figure out words; knowing the letters gives them the means to unlock them. If they know the sounds for *s, a,* and *t,* they have a good chance of being able to blend those sounds together into *sat.* Chinese children, on the other hand, have to learn intricate visual patterns and remember their details. If they do not memorize the word for apple, 苹果, there is little chance that they can unlock it from its parts.

During my early trips to China, another graduate student and I had long conversations with patient Xu Jian-yuan, one of my first research colleagues who was an English instructor in a teachers' college. He would never have said so, but I am sure he was astonished by how little we foreigners understood about the Chinese language. Self-effacing, with a ready smile, and a lock of hair that insisted on flopping down on his forehead, Xu had a manner that invited conversation. He would explain how Chinese characters are constructed and how they are taught. Every time we thought we understood, we had it wrong. Wasn't a character the same as a word? Weren't there any picture hints in characters? Why not, when all our beginning Chinese books showed characters as simplified pictures? How could you learn them? Why couldn't you sound them out?

Slowly we began to comprehend. Each Chinese character has much more detail than any of our 26 letters. To decode a character requires much more concentration. One small piece—a missing line or stroke, a missing dot—can change the meaning. Some characters differ by only one or two small strokes like 今 [jīn] *today* and 令 [lìng] *order.* Think of how one English letter can change the meaning of a word, for example, adding an "s" to "desert" becomes "dessert." Except in Chinese, a single character is made of five, ten, or as many as 15 essential lines called strokes.

There is no sound–symbol relationship as in English. There is no "sounding out" of characters. A character must be seen to understand it, and you either know what the character means, or you don't. That proved to be a very difficult concept to get into our Western heads. Each character has to be memorized. They contain only the vaguest of phonetic clues. There are no letters, I had to keep reminding myself. You cannot spell in Chinese; there are no letters. You cannot sound out a character. Period. It is not possible.

The classroom lessons I was observing in several Chinese cities kept reinforcing this. A year after meeting Xu, I made a five-hour train trip from Shanghai to his industrial city of Xuzhou to collect dissertation data and observe elementary school classes. He and I sat in on a first-grade lesson in a modest school. Children in jackets of yellows, reds, and greens were tucked together on small wooden benches. Orange and red ribbons festooned the girls' jet-black hair. We squeezed onto benches vacated by two students, who slid onto their neighbors' bench.

The teacher pointed to one of six characters on the blackboard.

"*Jin,*" she said, pointing to the first.

"*Jin,*" responded 60 first-graders.

"*Dao,*" she said, pointing to the second.

"*Dao,*" they repeated, strengthening their volume.

"Notice the strokes of this character; what do you know about it?" Hands shot up.

"Zhang Qian, you tell us." A rhythm was building: teacher, student; teacher, 60 students; teacher, student. On they went, deconstructing and rebuilding the characters, looking for familiar parts and noting new stroke combinations.

"Now practice them," directed the teacher. The children shifted a little in their benches and together drew the new characters in the air with their fingers, calling out a name for each stroke as they went— *shù, héngzhé, héng, héng, shùwangou.* Their loud voices accompanied emphatic finger movements, reinforcing the lesson that the strokes need to be written in the right order and the right direction—from top to bottom, left to right, inside to outside.

"The teacher has them study one character and its construction for five minutes," Xu said to me over the din.

"Five minutes?" I asked incredulously. "For one character?"

"They need to know what strokes are in it, the order they should be written in, how to balance them in the square, and the parts that can be confused with other characters," Xu explained.

Finally, the teacher curbed the cacophony of recitation and redirected the six-year-olds to the parts of characters that function somewhat like the root of a word in English. Several characters, for example, contain a component that means "water," and several insect names contain the segment for insect. She traced these components with fuchsia-colored chalk in three characters she had written on the board, exhorting the children to study them with their eyes and trace over identical ones in their textbooks. She then wrote similar looking characters on the board, retracing confusing strokes with the fuchsia chalk to remind them of other characters that differ by only one or two small strokes. Next the teacher had them read aloud a four-sentence story in their books, pressing them to pay attention to the characters. They read with gusto, but I was surprised that this class was over half way through first grade and they were only reading brief stories while American first-graders already would be able to read several pages of text.

I had originally gone to China in the winter of 1989–1990 to study early attempts at writing by two- and three-year-olds, what I called "prewriting," and to compare it to the prewriting of U.S. children. I wanted to see how the very young soak up knowledge about writing long before they are explicitly taught. The contrast was remarkable. The first child I watched "write" at Dragon Mountain Preschool in Nanjing left me and his teacher spellbound.

Chen Weili, my interpreter and research assistant that year, explained the procedures to the classroom aide, Ms. Liu, who was going to work with the children, since they knew her. I wanted them to try to write a letter to their auntie or their parents. We knew they were unlikely to be able to write characters, but we wanted to see what they might do when asked.

Ms. Liu, wearing a beige sweater buttoned against the classroom's winter chill and with her hair pulled back with a barrette, asked one child to select a pencil and she gave him a piece of paper.

"I don't know any characters," he said, his dark eyes focused on her face, tiny worry lines tugging at his lips.

"Just pretend to write something," she said gently. Gripping the little pencil, his thick padded jacket pressing against the desk, he made one small line. I could barely see it. Ms. Liu bent close to him and said something encouraging. He made another small mark and looked up. She urged him to continue. Next he made several interconnected lines, paused, and inched forward on his chair. He began to concentrate on writing, and we were mesmerized by his networks of tiny lines.

After a full minute, he put his pencil down and looked up at Ms. Liu. She spoke softly to him. He slid off the chair and trundled across the room to the teacher taking children back to their classroom, while another child started to "write." During the hour-long experiment, some children wrote longer, some almost nothing at all. On a later trip to China, I collected prewriting from 100 two- and three-year-olds for my dissertation, but I already knew what I'd find after the first prewriting attempts at the Dragon Mountain Preschool. Almost all the Chinese toddlers made short angular lines on a small section of the paper.

The prewriting samples I collected from preschoolers in several parts of the United States were very different. In one spacious Lenoir, North Carolina, preschool, a shy but energetic two-and-a-half-year-old girl, with bright barrettes clipped to her braids, pulled her small chair beside mine.

"Hi, there. Do you know how to write?" I asked, sticking as close as possible to the script we'd used in China. She looked down with a small, crooked smile and smoothed out a wrinkle in her shirt.

"Have you ever seen your mother or father write something?" Another small smile. She inched forward on her chair.

"My mother," she said softly.

I slid a sheet of paper to her. "Can you try to write a letter to someone? Can you pretend to write something?"

"I don't know how to write," she said. I smiled to myself. The Chinese children had said the same thing.

"That's okay," I said, "just pretend to write." She selected a short, thin pencil.

She carefully drew one line, stopped, and looked at it. Then without urging, she made another. She inched her fingers down the pencil and made large circular line after circular line. Looking at them, she added a few loops in blank spaces, handed the paper to me, then slid off the chair to join her classmates.

The difference between the prewriting of Chinese and American preschoolers was dramatic. Although it varied from child to child, none of the American children's writing was small and detailed like that of the Chinese youngster. Some of the U.S. three-year-olds made a shaky letter or two, often telling me that it was their name. Similarly, a few of the Chinese three-year-olds made attempts at characters. In general, though, the U.S. preschoolers made much larger marks and filled most of the space on the paper (see Figure 6.1).

It was obvious that children were soaking up elements of their national writing system long before entering school. In both countries, they are surrounded by written material—on store signs, buses, and cell phones, in the mail their parents read, in notes they write, and the text

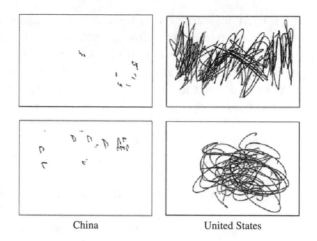

| China | United States |

Figure 6.1 Typical prewriting of Chinese and U.S. three-year-olds.

messages they send. From birth, Chinese children are surrounded by a complexity of strokes (see Figure 6.2). U.S. children are surrounded by much simpler forms (see Figure 6.3). In preschool and kindergarten, this is reinforced by teachers and textbooks.

By first or second grade, patterns are clearly set. To learn their language of unique and complex characters, Chinese children must focus on details unimaginable in the United States; American children learn sound patterns and how to use them in independent ways that are inconceivable to the Chinese. In each country, teaching methods are tailored to the language itself, and this directly affects the way we teach.

Yes, other dynamics are at play—social and physical environments, historical developments. But our writing systems are so embedded in

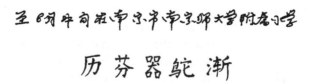

Figure 6.2 Chinese writing.

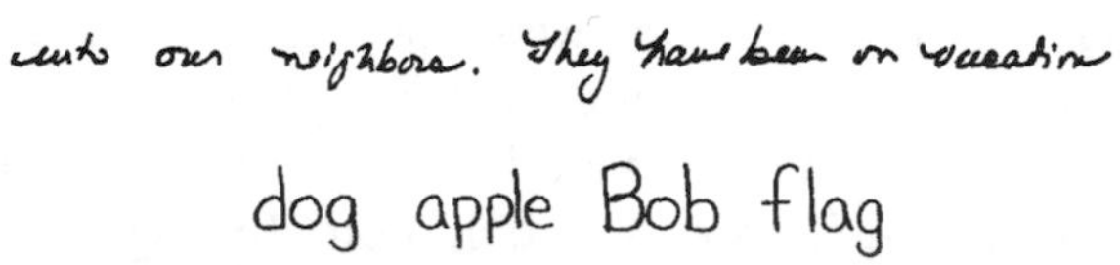

Figure 6.3 English writing.

everyday life—in what we see, what we do, what children notice—that they have a profound influence.

"Handmaiden to history, chronicler of the mind and the heart, writing is humankind's most far-reaching creation, its forms and designs endless," Cary Walingsky wrote in a 1999 *National Geographic* article on the evolution of written communication.[1] How true, and how early in life it begins.

7

Classroom Environment and Discipline

In elementary school classrooms across the United States, desks are usually clustered for collaboration and the walls are teaching spaces covered with learning materials and students' work. Teachers move around the room, often working with small groups while the rest study independently. In U.S. high schools, on the other hand, there is more teacher-centered instruction involving the whole class. Yet learning styles developed in earlier grades still shape interactions between student and teacher, and collaboration is common, especially on projects.

From the earliest grades in China, students sit straight and face the front of the room, where the teacher instructs the class and keeps a tight rein in a nonstop dialogue. Although some Chinese schools are beginning to introduce group work, the result is usually highly scripted. In general, there are no pauses or gaps during class time that might cause students' attention to wander. The classroom environments in the two countries are worlds apart, and those differences are intimately entwined with how students behave, focus, and learn.

I see it when I review my observation notes from Chinese classrooms. They are peppered with asides.

"No time for misbehavior."

"Too fast a pace for students to be off task."

"Kids sure have to be on their toes all the time."

"No lost motion between activities. None."

Nothing like my own classrooms where I sometimes stopped to make sure a student had the correct material out or to ask if a student's sprained ankle was getting better. Besides, my instructional day was interrupted constantly by phone calls from the office, school resource teachers and teaching aides coming to ask a question or borrow materials, and more.

Chinese lessons are choreographed. Teachers don't miss a beat through the entire 40-minute lessons in elementary school or high school. There are no phone interruptions from the office asking for a student to pick up materials, and no attendance to take or lunch count to tally. But there also are no discussions or responses to students' questions that may be off-topic, but important.

A fourth-grade language arts lesson in one rural school I visited in Anhui Province, a low-income area southwest of Shanghai, is typical of the steady, teacher-controlled pace. Not as fast-moving as many urban lessons I observed, it still maintained an underlying relentless progression.

Entering the classroom, Teacher Guo greeted the students seated at desks squeezed into a room bright with sunlight and the colorful hues of children's jackets and sweaters, but with bare walls. In his early thirties, his stride was relaxed, his face seemingly calm even though he was being observed by my research colleague, who was his former middle school teacher, and me. Using a video monitor on a metal cart (the only one in the school), he played a brief recording of birds, sheep, a cat, and a dog that accompanies their textbook and asked the class what the sounds reminded them of. He gestured to a student in the middle of the room.

The boy stood and responded, "Country scenery."

Pointing to another, the teacher asked, "What's your feeling about country scenery?"

"It makes you feel refreshed and close to nature," said another.

The teacher quickly introduced the textbook lesson about rural family life that they would study for the next several days, and wrote the word "refreshed" on the board. He then asked the class to find the two similar adjectives.

"Class, open your books and quickly find the two words. Please, do it quickly. Read the text paragraph by paragraph." The ten-year-olds riffled through the pages of their paperback textbooks hunting the words. Several hands went up.

"Song Zi-hao, you are the first to find the words."

"The textbook used the words *unique* and *fascinating*," Song Zi-hao said.

"*Unique* and *fascinating*," Mr. Guo repeated as he paced in the front of the classroom, a good-natured expression on his young face. "Tell us, where did you find them?"

"In Paragraph 7."

"Okay. *Unique* and *fascinating*, in the seventh paragraph, have you found them?" "Yes," they all responded as the teacher wrote the Chinese characters on the blackboard, then brushed chalk dust from his brown corduroy jacket.

"Read the sentence."

Fifty-five students read aloud, *For rural families, no matter when, no matter in which season, there will be unique and fascinating scenery.*

"*Unique* means different from others, and *fascinating* means the scenery is . . . " The teacher paused for the students to fill in the word.

" . . . beautiful."

"But in this sentence, the author also uses two other words before *unique* and *fascinating*."

"*No matter*," they all answered.

"*No matter*. Please read the two short phrases together."

They read aloud, *No matter when, no matter in which season.*

"Now do you understand *no matter when*?" he asked, pointing to a boy in the back. "Yes, you, Zhu Shuo,"

"It means, no matter if it's spring, summer, autumn or winter," the boy answered.

"If this one means 'no matter in spring, summer, autumn or winter,' then what about the next one?"

"It means 'in which season,' " answered several students. The teacher held the pace steady even though the subject matter had become complicated and the students were hesitating to answer.

"But then what does *no matter when* mean?" Back and forth. Question and answer. He led them incremental step by incremental step to extract the precise meaning of these few sentences, yet never slowing down. Once he was satisfied that most of the children understood, the teacher moved on rapidly, telling them how they should proceed to read the textbook story to understand it better. The students sat tall in their wooden chairs and read the two-page text aloud twice at their own speeds: They were asked to concentrate the first time on word meaning, the second time on the emotion in the words.

In the scores of lessons I have watched in China, the pace never lets up. There is a constant flow of teacher-controlled verbal give-and-take. Although current national curriculum standards call for moving away from teacher-dominated classrooms to allow more student initiative, including working in groups and connecting learning materials to students' lives, change has been incremental. Even in reform-minded schools that have introduced group work, the pace remains fast, the teacher in tight control.

In a second-grade language arts lesson at one Chinese urban school the teacher nodded to the class as she entered the room. The 32 students in this smaller-than-usual class stood to greet her then quickly sat down and opened their books. The teacher projected an image of their new vocabulary words on a large screen at the front of the room. All were animal names, which the students practiced reading aloud. The teacher then directed the class to form groups of four. The transition took seconds. The students were seated at double desks in pairs, so the two in front merely turned to face the two behind them. Each child in a group then selected a stick of a designated color from a jar—blue, green, red, or yellow—and the teacher assigned them the most specific tasks I have ever encountered in group work. This lesson was to practice standard Chinese pronunciation.[1]

"Students in each group please follow the order from green to red," she said. "Those with green sticks in each group will remind the rest of your group of the differentiation of /n/ and /ng/. Attention, students with the green sticks, please remind everybody of /n/ and /ng/. Then, you students with the yellow sticks, please remind us of retroflex and nonretroflex. The students with blue, please remind us of nasal sounds and lateral sounds. And those with the red sticks, you are the most awesome. I want to invite you to be our little teachers and lead us to read each new word twice."

I found out later that the stick color referred to the students' approximate ability to read characters—green being the strongest, red the weakest.

"Let's begin, and not too loud. Go."

For one minute the children in the eight groups rotated their tasks. Then she quickly drew their attention to her at the front of the room. Using a familiar pattern, she had them repeat the information to the whole class.

"First, I would like to ask someone with a green stick to teach the class. Lin Yu Qing," she said, calling on a tall girl in a bright turquoise jacket.

Standing, Lin Yu Qing called out, "*Da xiang* ends with a /g/. Please read after me."

"*Da xiang*," the class called back. "*Da xiang*."

Lin Yu Qing continued, "*Xian*, the first character of *xian he*, does not have a /g/ at the end. Please read after me."

"*Xian he. Xian he.*"

"*Kong*, the first character of *kong que*, ends with a /g/. Please read after me."

"*Kong que. Kong que.*"

One student after another led the class. After several rounds of the room, the teacher had everyone move back into position for a traditional lesson. That was it. No time spent moving chairs or deciding who in a group would do what, as is common with U.S. group work. No time for misbehavior, but also no decision-making by the students. The group work had lasted exactly six minutes and the students followed the teacher's precise instructions. They had no input into the process.

In junior and senior high schools, where Chinese teachers and students are consumed by exam preparation, group work and other techniques for student-centered learning appear to be nonexistent. Wang Xingye, the history teacher at a prestigious urban school in Guangzhou in southern China, summed up their teaching style: "I spend every minute of every class telling my high school students everything I know about history. Their job is to take notes and memorize the material."

In American classrooms, teachers occasionally lecture in the upper grades and students listen silently. But most times the teacher asks questions and students respond. It is far less formal than in Chinese classrooms. While Chinese teachers hunt for exact responses, teachers in the United States generally are gathering a collection of answers from the group. Even when a lesson is skill related and answers need to be specific, for instance, to suggest synonyms for *furious* or give concrete examples for a new word, such as *aggravate,* the back-and-forth discussion between teacher and student is much more casual than in China.

When they are working with the whole class, most U.S. teachers walk around the room and involve all the students. During one lesson in a large school on the southern edge of Los Angeles, I watched Ms. Moran, an effective fifth-grade teacher turn on a projector to display a set of questions on a screen. She then moved along the side of the room, asking students for answers, encouraging them to participate— sometimes by standing near them, at other times gesturing to them. She ended the lesson perched on an unused desk at the back of the room, while students continued to answer the questions on the screen at the front of the class. Although the focal point of a U.S. classroom might not be apparent to a visitor, and continues to shift, the students know where the teacher wants it to be—sometimes on the student speaking, sometimes on the screen, sometimes on the teacher. The teachers use a fluidity of movement and multiple communication techniques to keep students alert and engaged. In China they are almost always focused on the teacher.

Student movement also is assumed in the United States. Students move into groups, work with partners, and pass out materials at all grade levels. Elementary school children move to learning centers to gather material or to work, and they sit on the floor to play curriculum-related games or investigate books. They may move to the teacher for a small-group lesson or take a hall pass and go with a second child to the restroom. High school students work in groups, collaborate with partners, and seek materials and resources from other parts of the school. The teacher teaches the students the classroom routine and, when necessary, reminds them of behavior guidelines.

In one typical fourth-grade class at a crowded school in the middle of Los Angeles, the atmosphere is informal but purposeful. The teacher, Mr. Hammond, meets with a group of students seated on the rug around him, their books open to a story about how people communicate. Some others in the room work with partners writing questions about the theme of the month, communication. A few more students look for books on shelves along the wall. Still others are completing assignments at their desks.

After Mr. Hammond met with two groups for reading instruction, he had all the students return to their individual desks to work silently on an essay for a school contest. Later on, groups of three or four students worked on a long-term project about immigrant groups and what laws and rights affected their settlement. They brainstormed ideas about where to find information and assigned each member tasks. The teacher had given them a set of questions to consider as they developed the project and each was studying a different group—Russian, Mexican, Filipino, Korean, Guatemalan, and Chinese. The students had selected these five from the long list of immigrant groups in California because they decided they were the most important within their own neighborhoods. Mr. Hammond moved from group to group, making suggestions, reminding some to stay focused on the task, and answering questions. The students in his class understood what they needed to do, and when he was instructing one group, he kept an eye on the others to make sure they were working as they should, and the children knew it.

In American classrooms, individual students come and go—for special tutoring sessions to address learning disabilities or speech therapy, for trips to the library to investigate a topic, for restroom stops, and for orchestra practice. They also move in and out of lessons, sometimes missing parts, at other times catching up. This never happens in a Chinese classroom. There, teachers stand in the front of the room throughout the lesson, leaving at the end for the teachers' office or another class. Occasionally, schools testing more student-centered approaches may have students act out a skit from a text, form groups for a few minutes, or have a student walk to the classroom computer console to select an answer on the video screen. Otherwise the children must stay put. Bathroom breaks come only at the end of class.

During talks that I give about U.S. education to university students and educators in China I show lots of photos of typical American classroom scenes—students at different grade levels working in groups, children sitting on the floor listening to a guest speaker, and students and teachers discussing a chemistry experiment in a high school lab. When I first showed them, it was to a large audience at Yan'an University in north-central China. The opening photo, of children working in groups at round tables and one group off to the side with the teacher, brought a collective gasp from the 400 university students. Nearly half the audience took out their cell phones and photographed every classroom image I showed from then on. They had never seen anything so informal-looking in a school setting. I have since learned that images of clustered desks and students moving around the room and collaborating with each other stimulate Chinese audiences to ask, "Don't children misbehave when they have all that freedom?" Because Chinese teachers never sit down to work with students, it seems strange.

I tell them that U.S. teachers maintain discipline by being firm and also creating a relationship with their students. I tell them of methods such as a chart used by one third-grade teacher in an elementary school in northern California to help students maintain appropriate noise levels. It is a scale of 1–10 that is easy for children to understand. One is the sound of people breathing; two equals whispering; four, five, and six are appropriate work levels; seven is the permissible noise level during a class activity; eight verges on "danger," and so on. When they get too loud, she points to the desired level on the chart. There is no need for her to say anything.

But the informality runs counter to a prized Chinese value—discipline. China's long history of Confucian values and respect for education is an important influence on students' being focused on disciplined schooling. The structure and pacing of Chinese lessons leaves no time for misbehavior. In the United States, many new teachers as well as some with years of experience struggle to keep students on task, from being rude to each other or to the teacher, and from text-messaging friends. These are constant challenges. At the same time, American students—unlike their Chinese counterparts—are encouraged to add their own ideas during lessons and to express their opinions and insights in many ways. In China, students do not volunteer responses without being asked. They do not make suggestions to teachers. No second-grader asks, "Can we have another story today?" The teacher arrives in the classroom, greets the class, and the lesson begins—fast.

In the United States, when students are involved in their learning they tend not to misbehave. In recent years, however, as the emphasis on raising scores on achievement tests has grown, U.S. elementary classrooms have become more formal and the curriculum narrower. For almost a decade in many districts, reading and math in the elementary grades have been taught in tightly controlled subject matter programs provided by commercial textbook companies. Experienced teachers regard these new classrooms as deadly. Teacher frustration is high because their expertise is ignored.

"We're being turned into robots," complained one teacher after having even more curriculum eliminated to make way for tests to prepare for the standardized tests. "The kids are bored," she continued. "There's no time to encourage them to think deeply any more. You used to be able to see their love and enthusiasm for learning. Now you just watch the spark die as you tell them they have to take another test." Boring curriculum also generates discipline problems. In contrast, teachers using a hands-on science program found that discipline problems dropped significantly. Even the students most likely to misbehave wanted so much to do the science experiments that they controlled their impulses rather than miss out, said Jennifer Yuré, a former principal in the Pasadena, California, school district.

Yet even within the debilitating strictures of a test-laden curriculum, U.S. students still have more freedom to ask questions, to comment, and to move around the room than I have ever seen in a Chinese classroom.

Since my first trips to China in the 1990s, I have become keenly aware that Chinese students, from first grade on, are ready to respond in an instant to their teachers' questions. Every time I head for China, American teachers ask me to find out how teachers there produce students who are able to concentrate. I have discovered that in both countries, school discipline patterns are established early, even in preschools for those who attend them. What is expected and the ways to achieve those expectations set a tone for future schooling. U.S. preschool teachers generally expect young children to have a natural instinct for exploration, and they try to create a balance between encouraging them to experiment and investigate and guiding them to sit in groups, listen to stories, or have a brief lesson. They recognize that it takes time to develop acceptable social skills. Chinese preschool teachers are also cognizant of youngsters' limited attention spans and their need to move around and work with various materials. But when a class of 15 or 20 gathers to listen to the teacher, the children sit very still by most American preschool standards.

During an interview about parents' expectations for children, Zhou Dandan,[2] a mild-mannered graduate student, said her preschool son needed to learn to follow his teacher's instructions. "Otherwise he may become a troublemaker," she said.

"What would a troublemaker do?" I asked.

"Maybe when the teacher is instructing the class about something new or they are singing a song, a kid talks with other kids or they play with each other's feet or do not pay attention to the teacher."

"What if a child got up and left the class circle?" I inquired. "You know, and went to play with a toy or look at a book?"

She tilted her head back and laughed. "Oh, god. I don't think Chinese kids will do that. Maybe they don't follow the teacher's instructions, but they stay within themselves or they play with their neighbor."

My mind flashed back to a kindergarten class I had taught for a few months in southern California while the school hunted for a permanent teacher. Kindergartners are not my preferred age group, but I was sure I knew how to keep them busy. Instead, I struggled to keep those 30 little people focused and sitting on the rug in front of me at the beginning of each day. Most were cooperative, but a few kept bouncing up to do this and that—to get papers to pass out in order to "help me" or to get something from their lunch box to show the class when it was not time to do that. They were not "bad" children; they just had not yet learned to sit in a group and attend to what was going on. One girl kept getting up to play with blocks and puzzles. I had to sit her at my side to keep her still. This behavior wouldn't be tolerated in Chinese two-, three-, and four-year-olds. In the United States, we assume many children will need to learn how to behave appropriately, not only in preschool but also in kindergarten. In China, the behavior has already been learned. It is not unusual to see 30 three- and four-year-old preschool children sitting on chairs in a large circle for many minutes, waiting their turn. Although teachers and aides do oversee their behavior, the children just do not seem to have the impulse to move around like American children.

Much of this appears to be cultural. Research I have done about how children focus on objects suggests that long before they receive instruction in a class setting, two- and three-year-old Chinese children tend to look at smaller objects for longer periods of time, with less movement, than do U.S. children.[3] Although Chinese children may display this early ability to concentrate on one thing, their primary-grade teachers do not leave attentive behavior to chance. Huang Ren Song, a specialist in early childhood education at Nanjing Normal University, says that beginning in first grade, teachers use continuous encouragement to help children concentrate. For the first several days of the school year, the teachers show children how to sit down, how to hold a pencil, how to listen and work, how to walk in the classroom, and how to stand in line. Through demonstrations, stories, and games, they teach proper school behavior and they regularly criticize the children's work so they will learn to improve. They also regularly tell parents how their child needs to improve.

Once the parent of a new first-grader showed me five text messages she had received on her phone that day from her daughter's teachers—three from the math teacher, two from the language arts teacher. One of them had also spoken to her in person about her daughter's off-task behavior. This level of communication is typical for many Chinese teachers. Some of the messages are communal, sent to all parents, and others are for individual students. By junior high school, the number of messages increases with the added number of subjects and teachers.

Many Chinese parents and university educators have told me that teachers are very hard on students and often use shame as a means of discipline, ridiculing those who do not know their lessons. One language teacher for adults whose child was in upper elementary school said, "They sometimes speak very impolitely to students and show their anger if a student makes a mistake." This, she added, is considered good because strict teachers produce very good students. Some Chinese parents disagree, but say this is a commonly held belief.

No matter how the teachers may behave, showing respect for one's parents and teachers has been ingrained in Chinese culture for many hundreds of years, since the times of Confucius. Parents and students may not always like what teachers do or say, but they are respected and, occasionally, feared. Said one parent, "We consider the teachers to be like our parents because they have a lot of knowledge and power."

Criticism, not praise, is the norm from Chinese teachers. Once while I was traveling to the airport with an English instructor in Nanjing, she received several text messages from her junior high school son's teachers telling her how he could improve. I asked if they ever texted congratulations about students' improvements.

"Never," she said.

"And if they have won first prize in a contest?" I asked.

"Then they say the student must try even harder so he can beat students from other schools."

This highlights the very different expectations that prevail in the two educational systems. In American classrooms of all types—whether strict and traditional or extremely interactive—"why" and "how" are valued questions. Why do cars make smog? Why do "s" and "c" sometimes make the same sound? How do worms move? The teacher may not know the answer, but accepts and often encourages this type of inquisitiveness. Student suggestions to a teacher are also respected, and teachers who encourage student interaction are considered better than those who just follow a script. Even in more test-oriented classrooms, teachers expect more student initiative than do their Chinese counterparts. More than one Chinese parent who has an imaginative child has told me their child would fare better in an American school because it would allow him or her more freedom. A Shanghai principal who spent time shadowing the principal of Malibu High School in southern California wrote a book after returning home in which he extolled the openness and interaction he saw between the Malibu High students and teachers.[4]

Many middle-class parents in China, aware of the differences in schooling offered in other countries, are torn between their desire to see their children learn in a less stringent, more imaginative atmosphere and the realization that their children must pass the highly competitive national college entrance exams if they are to have a chance at a good university education and have good job prospects. On the other hand, many U.S. teachers and parents say they would like to see their students more focused on academic work and better behaved in class, even as they develop critical thinking skills and learn to take the initiative. The dilemma, then, is how do we achieve the best of both worlds?

8

Digging Deep

Worming my way into a desk in the back corner of a crowded Los Angeles classroom, I nodded to the teacher, who had just settled his fourth-grade students after their morning recess. I was visiting a series of U.S. classrooms in 2011 to keep myself current. This nearly windowless room, a "temporary" modular structure that stands apart from the main school buildings and is anything but temporary, was depressing. It was a brisk and sunny spring day, but it was hard to tell in this room.

The teacher, Mr. Jacobsen, projected a vocabulary review worksheet onto a screen, a potentially deadly exercise. But his strong, congenial voice corralled the restive ten-year-olds. All 30 children seated at pushed–together double desks were attentive. He pointed to the first word on the screen and read it aloud.

"Stethoscope. Say it."

"Stethoscope," came the forceful response.

The teacher walked to the bulletin board and picked up a photograph of one.

A girl in the middle of the room raised her hand. "Jessica?" he asked, inviting her to speak.

"I went to the doctor last week and she used one of those," the girl said.

I had just returned from China and was jolted by her comment. In a Chinese school, a student would never jump into a teacher-led activity to relate his or her personal experience.

"Right, did it feel cold?," he asked. "Sometimes the metal and plastic on it are cold."

Jessica nodded and smiled.

"What is it used for?"

"It listens to your heart?"

Mr. Jacobsen nodded to her and read the word *stethoscope*, and its definition, aloud. Most of the students joined him.

"Next word. Superstition. Say it."

"Superstition," they responded in unison.

"Some people think that 13 is an unlucky number," the teacher said. "Why is 13 thought to be an unlucky number? Why not 20, or 40?" A few students started talking to each other.

"Raise your hand and tell us why." He nodded at a girl near the back of the room and moved closer to hear her soft voice.

"Because one time when I passed a house with a 13 number I fell off my bike," she said.

"So you had bad luck with it? So you've heard that the number 13 is unlucky? Who told you it was unlucky?"

Another student blurted out, "*Friday the 13th,* the movie." The students were drawing almost entirely from personal experience and conjecture, and that was the teacher's purpose—to have them make individual connections to help them bring the words to life, and to remember them.

"Any other things you've heard that are unlucky to do?" the teacher asked. Hands waved, the children were begging to be called on. "Manuel."

"Go past a ladder," the boy said.

"Right, it's bad luck to walk underneath a ladder." The teacher was careful to model appropriate wording rather than criticize the students, believing that too much criticism and correction could discourage their willingness to speak up in class.

He moved to the side of the room. "All right, tell your partner some other superstitions you have heard." They all turned to students near them and jabbered away, some gesturing furiously. The teacher quickly drew their attention back to him.

"What other superstitions do you know? Maria?"

"Breaking a mirror."

"Ah, seven years' bad luck for breaking a mirror, right? Alma."

"Stepping on a crack in the sidewalk."

"Yeah. You have to step over the crack. Vanessa?"

On they went, enthusiastic about contributing to the class ideas. He wrapped it up, "What are they called?"

"Superstitions," the whole class responded.

Part of their homework was to make a list of all the superstitions they know. The teacher walked back to the projector and pointed to the next word.

Not only was the environment more relaxed in this classroom than those I'd seen in China, but the teacher's expectations also were different. Although this vocabulary exercise took only a few minutes, he expected the students to talk about their own experiences, to give their opinions and ideas, and to risk being wrong. Talking about their experiences helped them understand and remember the new words in their reading text.

The differences between U.S. and Chinese classrooms are obvious in some ways: the environment, a jumble of desks versus neatly arranged ones; small versus large class sizes; and informal versus formal interactions. More subtle, but equally as important, though, is how American teachers draw students and their experiences into the learning process. No matter what the teaching style—and there are many in the United States, from very strict and formal to very relaxed—this is a hallmark of American education.

The U.S. teacher's role in reading and writing lessons is to provide children with a variety of opportunities to immerse themselves in the learning process, to make sense of it, and gradually to understand how to use these skills to gain knowledge and express themselves and their opinions with clarity. In China, the teacher's role is primarily to help students dig deeply into the meaning of a text, to understand in depth and detail what the author is saying, and almost never to help the students express what they may think or feel about the text they had read.

A common method used in American schools to help students make sense of a text is to first connect the story or article to their individual experiences, then later have them connect that story or article to other texts, and, finally, to larger issues in the world. A decade or so ago, I sometimes saw small posters in classrooms that said, "Text to self, text to text, text to world."[1] The posters are now gone, but the teaching strategy has become embedded in teacher practices no matter what reading program they use.

I have watched this process of making connections unfold in American classrooms for years.

In Esmeralda Ortiz's first-grade classroom in the heart of Los Angeles, 23 children sat at individual desks, some facing forward toward the white board, the rest facing the center of the spacious room. A bank of large windows let in the early morning light as eager, active children settled down. The walls, covered with students' work, reading program charts and posters, and charts from class discussions, not only enlivened the room but also were an integral part of the teaching process. She finished taking attendance and began an introductory lesson of a folktale about an ant who wants to see the sky, so he climbs ever taller plants and trees until he realizes the futility of his effort.

The students pulled out their large, hardback reading books filled with a collection of stories designed to engage them and teach them decoding and comprehension skills. The books are twice as large as those in a Chinese classroom, and the children are not allowed to write in them or take them home. Yet the contents are similar in both countries—a variety of fiction and nonfiction stories and poems, often organized into themes, such as transportation, communication, and so on.

"What's your favorite folk tale?" she asked the class. Several of the children were just beginning to learn English.

"The Three Little Pigs," said an enthusiastic boy in a T-shirt emblazoned with a cartoon character. The teacher moved near his desk to encourage him.

"Oh, The Three Little Pigs. What did you like about it?"

"I like when the wolf can't blow down the house."

Other hands shot up, and several students talked about the folktales they liked. She then had them hunt for words in the story they did not recognize or understand. One was *dandelion*.

The day before, in preparation for reading "The Way of the Ant" and to give all of these urban children a shared nature experience, the teacher had taken the class to the school garden where they found dandelions, some with flowers and some with puffy seeds to blow. They also looked at the different heights of the plants and trees, to get a visual understanding necessary to comprehend the ant's efforts. She had them talk about the garden experience in class and relate what they had seen to the photos of dandelions and trees she had brought to class. Before beginning to read the story, they looked at an illustration in their books of the ant climbing a dandelion.

Ms. Ortiz moved the class into a circle on the rug, and she joined them on the floor. They began reading the story aloud with her, figuring out words by using alphabetic, phonetic, and contextual clues. It is a process adult readers do automatically, but for some first-graders it is arduous.

It was slow-going as she helped children follow the words. Some didn't know enough English yet to read and understand much of the vocabulary. They got the gist of the story because they were reading it aloud and seeing the pictures, but learning to read in a new language was difficult.

After four pages, Ms. Ortiz stopped them. "So why is the ant changing the things he is climbing?" She turned back a few pages. "He climbed the grass and then the dandelion and then the rose. And now he's climbing the sunflower." The students all seemed to understand. They read several more pages and she stopped them again.

"Let's make a connection to our own lives. Who has ever felt like the ant? Have you ever been in a situation like the ant?" An eager boy's hand went up. He rocked forward on his knees, talking excitedly.

"When I first moved here I didn't know about tall buildings and when I went into them I wanted to get up higher and see what they were like. They made me feel weird." Ms. Ortiz suggested he remember that valuable idea because the next day they would all write an ending to the sentence, "This story reminds me of how I feel when _____."

Pointing to the page where the ant has climbed a huge tree, she asked how it must feel. They all wanted to say something.

"Tired."

"Excited."

"Ready to sleep."

"Have you ever been tired like the ant?" Up went more hands. She looked for someone who didn't usually contribute in the large group, but time was running out, so she called on the more self-assured children.

"When my dad works hard on the exercise bike, he gets sweaty."

"I did a challenge ride on my scooter, in a race."

"Yeah, what the ant is doing is like running a race," said Ms. Ortiz to help tie the child's example more closely to the story.

Moving between reading the book and talking about the students' lives comes naturally to Esmeralda Ortiz and most American teachers. The reading program she was using, which many school districts mandated to be taught in rigid ways, usually has teachers devote a lot of time to discrete skills and vocabulary development that often go beyond many students' abilities. However, the stories themselves come with questions that are open-ended. The teacher editions also include multiple ways to connect the stories to the students' lives that most teachers already know instinctively.

The Chinese government launched new curriculum standards at the beginning of the twenty-first century as part of a far-reaching reform plan to stimulate innovation and imagination among its future leaders by requiring more real-world, student-centered teaching, adopting more Western methods. In 2001, the education ministry issued one of its periodic directives, the Guideline for Curriculum Reform of Basic Education, which, like most such policies, had been sent out to various education committees and provinces for comment before the final version was released.[2] It calls for "an end to over-emphasis on imparting book knowledge," which is "often too difficult or elaborate for students to learn, and sometimes simply out of date."[3] It required more inter-active learning in the schools and teachers were expected to connect lessons to children's life experiences. Students, the Ministry of Education said, needed to take a more active part in learning, rather than simply learning from lectures and repetition.

After this directive was released, China introduced more engaging textbooks. Math books demonstrate ways that concepts are used in everyday life. Language arts books include stories that students can relate to, plus activities to reinforce those lessons. For instance, an ancient tale about chariot travel is accompanied by suggested extra activities that illustrate how students and adults travel today. I have not seen this approach used much, though. In my experience, it would almost never occur to Chinese teachers to ask students to relate their everyday experiences to story ideas or characters. Such strategies have never been part of Chinese education traditions. More than one Chinese parent has told me that if their children ever wrote what they really thought for their assignments, they would be reprimanded.

Instead, Chinese teachers lead students to dig deeply into under-standing the texts. The goal is to help students comprehend the details of stories, as well as the techniques used by the author and, when appro-priate, the motives of characters or an underlying moral. Lessons are built almost entirely around the text, and student comments are nearly always tied directly to the author's words. The students learn to probe the material through tightly knit lessons comprised of one question after another from the teacher. Although parents lament the amount of memorization and the lack of innovation endured by students, most Chinese learners display good subject matter understanding.[4]

While watching Chinese teachers in action over the years, I have been fascinated by how they teach reading.

"Amazing repetition," I wrote in a letter to one of my Chinese research partners, Zhang Feng, in the 1990s. "It's hard to believe how much repetition there is in a lesson." I had just read transcripts from my observations of first- and second-grade language arts classes. The margins of my notes from these sessions are scattered with com-ments. "Students just read the same paragraph four times." "They've read it so many times, the class must have memorized this story by now."

Feng was amused at my reaction. He assured me that this was normal in China, and that it was the best way for children to learn to read and understand Chinese.

But was it, I wondered, just memorization and repetition for repeti-tion's sake? I knew that it was important to implant the complex Chinese language characters in children's heads, that without repetition they are virtually impossible to learn. But what does repetition and detailed focus do for comprehension, I wondered? It must have value, I thought, and be more than just a mindless, rote activity, as some Westerners have characterized Chinese teaching methods.

One second grade lesson I had mentioned to Feng was at Chang Jiang School in Nanjing, discussed briefly in Chapter 6. On a warm spring day in 1996, Qiu Wei, my research assistant and interpreter, and I watched from small children's chairs at the back of the classroom. Wang Jing, described as a very good and experienced teacher by both Qiu Wei and the school's director, stood on a slightly raised platform at the front of the room, with 55 children facing her from their desks arranged in cramped rows.

"They're studying a poem about Yellow Mountain in Anhui Province," Qiu Wei said. The mountain, which is about a ten-hour bus ride from Shanghai, is regarded as sacred and is visited by many tourists. Qiu Wei whispered that the students had probably already studied the poem for homework. Teacher Wang began.

"Yellow Mountain has been famous throughout the world for its hot springs, special rocks, strange pine trees, and sea of clouds. Today we are going to learn a text that is about Yellow Mountain. Wang Lei, please read the title of this text."

"Special Rocks of Yellow Mountain."

"Good. The whole class together, read the title aloud."

"Special Rocks of Yellow Mountain," they read together, loudly.

"Then which element of Yellow Mountain is this text about?"

Student hands went up. She gestured to one. "This text is about the special rocks in Yellow Mountain."

"Right. I'll ask another student to answer my question." More hands went up. "You, please." She motioned to another.

"This text is about the special rocks in Yellow Mountain."

"All right. It's about rocks in Yellow Mountain. But what kind of rocks?"

"Special," they all chorus.

"Yes. They are all special rocks. With the help of the pictures in our textbooks, we learn that this text is about the special and fantastic rocks in Yellow Mountain."

A few minutes into the lesson and I was already stunned—and numbed—by the repetition. The students heard every phrase, every sentence at least three times, usually more.

Teacher Wang had all 55 students read the text, aloud, more or less in unison.

"Now please answer my question. How many kinds of special rocks are mentioned in the text? Please answer the question loudly." She called on a boy near us.

"There are The Deity Peach, A Monkey Watching the Sea, A Deity Directing the Way, A Cock Crowing at Dawn, and so forth."

"Is this answer complete enough?"

"Not complete enough," said several students.

"Besides The Deity Peach, A Monkey Watching the Sea, A Deity Directing the Way, and A Cock Crowing at Dawn, are there other special rocks? Chen Na, you answer please."

"There are A Dog Watching the Moon, A Lion Clinging to a Ball, A Fairy Playing on the Strings."

"The combination of the answers of two students is the complete answer to the question," said Wang. Qiu Wei whispered to me that the teacher's response helped children read accurately and closely. But I found it frustrating, especially for teaching second-graders.

Wang then told the children there were three things to notice while she read the poem aloud—the pronunciation of difficult characters, the pauses between sentences, and the special nature of the rocks. She read the whole text. At the end Qiu Wei leaned over and said, "She reads beautifully. When students learn excellent pronunciation and intonation, it helps them comprehend the text."

"Next, we'll learn the text step by step," Teacher Wang told the students. She began with the first picture and then the first paragraph, moving methodically through the text, paragraph to paragraph, sentence to sentence, being careful to examine every new word and phrase and ensure it was understood. The first paragraph was comprised of two sentences stating where Yellow Mountain is located and the fact that unusual rocks are found there. By the time she finished, they had probably read the words aloud four or five times, certainly enough to have memorized them and internalized the author's rhythm.

Wang moved on to the second paragraph, which had only one sentence. Analyzing it and the picture took another five minutes.

"There is only one sentence in the second paragraph. What does it tell us? Shu Feng, please." She pointed to a boy in the front row whose dark blue jacket was zipped to his chin.

"The second sentence tells us . . . "

"There is only one sentence," the teacher said, jumping in when the boy paused. "Why the second one?"

Wow, I thought. Just as the Chinese parents had told me, students must be on their toes every moment in order not to be embarrassed. These are second-graders! The boy responded instantly.

"It has two meanings. One is that the Deity Peach is like a big peach. The other is . . . " He hesitated.

The teacher jumped in again. "The answer is not complete enough. Who will have another try? What does the only sentence tell us? Hu Jia, please." She was pacing energetically in front of the class.

"It has two meanings. One is that the Deity Peach is like a big peach falling from the sky."

Wang repeated the student's words, "The Deity Peach is like a big peach falling from the sky. It talks about the rock's origins and its big size, so it talks about the rock's . . . "

"Shape," several responded.

"Yes, it talks about the rock's shape. And what about the second meaning? Sun Jing, please."

"The second one is that it has fallen to the stone ledge at the top of the mountain."

"So it talks about the rock's . . . " She paused for the student to continue.

"It tells us where the rock is located."

"So it talks about the location of the Deity Peach," Wang repeated. "The paragraph has two meanings. One is the shape of the rock and the other is the location, but she has missed one point. Who can add to her answer? The sentence has three meanings of the rock."

"The third one is that it tells us the name of the rock."

"Yes, the sentence also tells us the name of the rock. It first tells us the name, then the shape, and the location. There are three meanings in one sentence."

When the lesson had ended 20 minutes later, I felt exhausted—and distressed. The teacher's control of the questions and answers did not feel right. Only a few students had a chance to respond, and even then they were often criticized. They were given no chance to connect to their own ideas or experiences that I could see. Although both Qiu Wei and the director had described Wang as an excellent teacher, I could not understand why. The students had been led to every morsel of information from the sentences and paragraphs.

Over the next several years, I continued to probe this method and began to wonder about the general practice of reading aloud. On Chinese high school and college campuses, I watched students bend over their books, walking and reciting aloud, memorizing texts. There is a Chinese saying educators often quote when I ask about this practice: "If you read or recite a book one hundred times, the meaning of the book will come out naturally." (读书百遍, 其义自见; *Du shu bai bian, Qi yi zi xian.*) This belief was common centuries ago, and clearly it continues to be an essential part of China's pedagogical practices. For many, the repeated readings emphasize the beauty and cadence of the language and help the reader uncover its meaning.

In China the teaching of literacy has remained essentially the same for more than 2,000 years. Dynasties may have varied, but most literacy training remains unchanged. It reflects the thinking of ancient Chinese educators.[5] As Zhu Xi (1130–1200) suggested 1,000 years ago in his work on reading methods, oral recitation not only helps memorization but also aids comprehension. He wrote:

> In reading, keep the curriculum small but the effort you make on it large. . . . Understand them [the texts] in every detail, recite (*du song*) them until you are intimately familiar with them. . . . In this way those with weak memories naturally will remember and those without the power of comprehension will be able to comprehend.[6]

He continues:

> The value of a book is in the recitation (*du*) of it. By reciting it often, we naturally come to understand it . . . If we recite it again and again, in no time the incomprehensible becomes comprehensible and the already comprehensible becomes even more meaningful.

Reading in ancient China was taught through two processes: *nianshu,* the reading aloud of texts in order to divide them into sentences and paragraphs and convert them to meaning, since they had no punctuation, and *jiangshu,* the explication of the meaning.[7]

He Lun, a well-known scholar who lived in the Ming era (1368–1644), explained in instructions for his family the interaction between teacher and student through *jiangshu*: "The key of text-explanation is that after [the teacher's] explanation, you should look carefully, study intently, ponder quietly, interpret sentence by sentence, and comprehend paragraph by paragraph. Only in this way can one get the main idea."[8]

Six hundred years ago it was common for the teacher to interrupt the student for further clarification and to admonish him to heed the teachings. These habits of *jiangshu* remain deeply engrained today, and twentieth-century efforts to alter them have proven frustrating. In 2009, Yu Zhenyou, my research partner from China Women's University in Beijing, and I participated in a lesson critique in a rural school in Anhui Province, 150 miles west of Shanghai. The school is located near his hometown, and when time permits, he helps its teachers with their education strategies. In attendance at the after school meeting were several language arts teachers, including the one who had taught the demonstration lesson we had all watched, as well as the school principal. Following up on a comment of mine about comprehension strategies, Yu spoke passionately:

> Nancy mentioned two types of comprehension. The first type is to understand the original meaning of the phrase. The second type can be interpreted as "each person has a different understanding of the phrase." In English, the two types are defined as "make meaning of" and "make sense of." I suggest that you note down the two phrases. Both phrases can be translated into "理解" [understand] in Chinese, but they are quite different.

He went on to explain to the group that the term "make meaning of" was similar to what they did in their classrooms—having students understand the dictionary meaning of words and phrases. From a different perspective, the term "make sense of" means that every individual has a unique way of comprehending a text. To him the word *uniqueness* relates to a scene from his personal experiences, but to someone else it might trigger an entirely different scene or idea.

In that way, he said, phrases can be shown to carry broader meanings. He asserted that Chinese teachers now need to focus on teaching the students to relate the phrase to their already-existing experiences. They need to understand not only individual phrases, he said, but also the full texts in relation to their own experiences.

But Yu said that understanding texts in this way should not mean throwing out all traditional Chinese education methods. The ancient methods, such as recitation, have value. "If the language is beautiful, why not recite it? A good text should be recited. In the process of reciting a good text, sensitivity to the language can be constructed. It helps us understand when something is said awkwardly, and when it is said beautifully." Western educators, he added, overemphasize "making sense of" at the expense of deep meaning and the beauty of language.

When I suggest to American teachers and other Western educators that our methods of teaching focus much more on the personal meaning of an idea or story to the reader than Chinese teaching, they agree, and then add that we often spend too little time discussing and comprehending the author's concepts. The Chinese, as Yu pointed out, always dig into a text. Their students know much more about the author's intentions, but they do not learn how those might relate to their lives or the world they live in.

In classrooms and schools in many provinces throughout China, I have watched the way lessons plumb phrase after phrase for a writer's meaning and at the same time highlight beautiful language. This occurs even in schools that have begun to emphasize the new curriculum that urges teachers to involve students actively in classroom learning. One of the clearest examples I have observed was a well-executed lesson in 2011 at an urban school, where fourth-grade students had learned how to work effectively in a group—taking over part of the teaching process and even engaging the rest of the class. But the way the children explored and explicated the text was almost identical to the teacher-led lessons I watched in the early 1990s. Explication and close reading dominated; connections to the students' lives or ideas were missing.

The fourth-graders were reading "I'm Not the Weakest," a story about a picnicking Russian family that is surprised by a rainstorm. The mother offers the only raincoat to her youngest child, Sasha, who is insulted by the offer and uses it to protect a beautiful flower, which she views as the weakest among them.

The children were divided into groups, with each group taking a paragraph or two to read and analyze. The leader of the first group stood before the class, the rest of the group seated around him.

"Let's first look at the first paragraph, the paragraph that starts with *It's a holiday with oppressively hot weather . . .* "

"Let's invite Huang Hao Ran to read it for us beautifully," the leader continued.

Huang Hao Ran read, "*It was a holiday with oppressively hot weather. A family went to the forest: father, mother, Toria, a fifth-grade student, and the four-year-old Sasha.*"

The leader continued, "This paragraph tells us that a four-person family went on a holiday, and it tells the time, weather, place, and the relationship among the four persons. The weather is oppressively hot. The author does not write this randomly. There is some reason. Let us invite Liu Xiang to explain it."

Liu Xiang stood and said, "You know the weather is oppressively hot, which means it's going to thunder and rain. Here the author writes 'oppressively hot weather' to foreshadow the climax of the story."

The leader interjected, "Now we stop here for a while. Does anybody want to add an explanation to this paragraph? Wu Zi."

Wu Zi, another group member, began, "I have two explanations to add. First, I want to add something to Liu Xiang's comments. The weather is oppressively hot, which means it's fine and clear, comfortable. So the family was not prepared and only brought one raincoat.

That foreshadows the story end. Second, the author points out the relationship between the two children. Toria is in grade five and Sasha is four years old and much younger. The author writes this in order to explain why the mother gave the raincoat to Sasha first."

The teacher stepped in to guide the discussion. "The raincoat is given to the weakest. The title of the text is 'I'm not the weakest.' So mother gave the raincoat to the weakest, Sasha, right? You have noticed the relationship between them. Very good." The group interrupted her, partially through their body language and also because the leader, an enthusiastic, strong-willed boy, was anxious to continue.

He offered an observation about certain words in the text that have special sounds. The remaining groups continued, each analyzing a paragraph or two, all in the same fashion, and all reminiscent of 1990s lessons. The student participation made for a much livelier class dynamic compared with the earlier lessons I'd observed. It also seemed to encourage them to think more about the text and about the writer's style. But the focus on the literal meaning of words, the details, and the author's craft was the same. U.S. teachers would encourage the students to ask, "Why did this character do *x*?" or "What else could *y* have done?" From time to time in this Chinese class, the groups drew a moral from a story, but the students' opinions and conjecture, and any connection to their own experiences were missing.

Back in Los Angeles, I continued to probe the differences and similarities between the two countries' ways of approaching language arts. Once again I was struck by the contrast between the Chinese approach—parsing words and sentences, to help children understand the specifics of the writing by digging more deeply—and the American tendency to react to writing through conjecture, personal experiences, and the reader's ideas.

Adults tend to agree. One man, who works to strengthen his granddaughter's academic skills, told me he was impressed by her thoughtful writing generated by an essay she had read. On further investigation, however, he discovered that although the beginning of the author's essay had sparked a thought-provoking response from her, she had missed his main point because she had reacted personally too early.

This tendency of American teaching to move too quickly from the text to real-life application can even be seen in the way students are prepared for the popular SAT college exam. In an online preparation site, an essay that was given a high grade was specifically praised for its connection to the writer's personal experience, but was not penalized at all for nearly ignoring the main thesis of the writing prompt.[9]

In a Los Angeles charter school, where teachers are free to design their own curriculum to meet state standards, two teachers shared a fourth- and fifth-grade combination class of 60 students. They planned a year of instruction that integrated science and math, language arts and social studies. I visited their class several times throughout the year as the students read and then wrote ecologically focused mysteries and studied biomes, often referred to as ecosystems, and other science concepts about biodiversity.

On one morning visit, Tandra Selva, the teacher who specialized in language arts, gathered a group of ten students who were reading an eco-mystery, a story of a scientific investigation and a mystery wrapped into one. This one involved fireflies and ravens. She told the children that she hadn't read the book, that they needed to describe for her what had happened in the first three chapters, which they had read on their own. Her intent was to get them to be specific about what they were learning in the novel. Mariah, a talkative student with shoulder-length red hair and a mischievous smile, began by describing the characters and the initial action in the book. Others helped out when she forgot important details.

"So is that the mystery?" Ms. Selva asked of Mariah's description. Several students chimed in at once.

"Put your hands up. You'll all have a chance to speak, but I'm really happy you all want to say something."

Kenneth, a tall, energetic boy, said, "In chapters one, two and three, there are different times the characters see the crows."

"Ravens," several students corrected. A few voices added, "Ravens are scary." "I don't like them." "They're five times bigger than other birds."

"They are huge," Ms. Selva agreed. She explained that ravens have a bad reputation because they are scavengers.

The conversation shifted to what the landscape in the novel is like. They'd had some beginning instruction on biomes, but not much. A girl near the teacher, leafing through her book, said she thought the important biome in the story is in the mountaintops because the main character is obsessed with going there.

"Yeah, I think she's partially right, but there are meadows too," said another student. "And you can see the mountains from the meadows." They were way off in their understanding of a biome, but the teacher did not tell them that. Instead she led them to think about the clues they had unearthed so far and to make some early guesses about the land and its association with the mystery. Over the next several days, they would refine and develop their knowledge of biomes and which ones played a role in the eco-mystery.

Unlike the two Chinese classes that were digging for specific clues in the words the author wrote, the Los Angeles students talked about how the author was developing the storyline, what the author might say next, and how she would resolve the mystery. The teacher was leading them to conjecture and to gradually support their ideas with facts.

During the afternoon science lesson the other teacher of the combination class introduced a biomes research project that would be due in two weeks. Each child was asked to select a biome. Michelle Rosier, who specializes in math and science instruction, handed out an assignment sheet that described the project, explained what biomes are, and more. After 10 minutes spent answering their questions, she stopped the students. "Let's get you researching now. You have more questions than answers, so today you are going to begin by finding out about different biomes." She pointed to a list of websites on the assignment sheet and then quickly introduced one on a laptop. The students picked up laptops from the school cart and began navigating the Internet to hunt for material, helping each other in the search. Ms. Rosier walked from one child to the next, troubleshooting, proposing new ways to search, and answering more questions.

Both the Chinese classes that tried group work and the Los Angeles charter school class are more ambitious and have a flexibility that their regular counterparts do not enjoy. The Chinese experimental classes have half as many students as a regular Chinese school, and the Los Angeles charter school is free of its district's straightjacket curriculum. Even so, it is apparent that fundamental cultural characteristics survive. The Chinese, even in a newly restructured classroom environment, still value and practice digging deeply into texts and side-step students' experience and opinions. The Americans concentrate on students' opinions and reactions to stories and do not mine the text or study the language of the writer in the depth the Chinese do. We might want to adapt some of each other's practices to augment our own.

9

Performance and Improvisation

Zhang Feng, one of my earliest research partners, lived for a year in Alhambra, California, during 1997. He and I had developed a level of trust that allowed us to be pretty honest when something bothered us about each other's country. His email describing a children's soccer tournament still makes me laugh when I re-read it today. It pinpoints so well a major difference between our cultures.

When an American friend took him to the Rose Bowl stadium in Pasadena to watch children from five to eight years of age compete, Feng wrote that he felt he had landed on another planet. He described the young soccer players entering the stadium in their teams.

> Appalling to me as a Chinese viewer was the free, casual, and hustling-bustling style of the whole scene: hundreds of banners of different colors and sizes and shapes carrying the names of the teams. Each seemed to be competing in its uniqueness and even weirdness—Green Lizards, Yellow Tigers, Wide Turtles, Roaring Lions, Blue Dolphins, Grasshoppers. The little soccer players in rather randomized manner roamed and floated along in a zigzagging stream into the center of the stadium. Few seemed to care about the marching music roaring from the loudspeakers, which could have brought them into the stadium in somewhat neat steps. From time to time, a fizz stirred among the parents, grandparents, and friends that sent shouts, screams, whistles, and laughter into the air as their children or an adored team came into sight.

He contrasted this to similar sports meets at his daughter's school in China. The children are neatly lined up, he said, and "when they march into the scene you see a flow of neatly cut squares, almost equally spaced, and all trying to follow the marching music." Each team is led by someone holding a sign or a flag showing its name, but none are strikingly unique and they are all the same color, shape, and size, which, he pointed out, contributed "to the rather disciplined overall structure of the scene." He added—rather longingly, I thought—

> Onlookers, including parents, quietly watch the parade. An applause may be the only sound heard from the crowd as a greeting and encouraging gesture to each team. The parents feel happy and proud of their children, and even excited, but all these reactions seem to happen inwardly.

Feng's description reminded me of the first elementary school lessons I'd observed in Xuzhou, China, in 1991. I was fascinated by the teacher's careful organization of the lesson and by each child's ability to speak clearly to a large group. It was nearly a performance and made my own teaching methods suddenly appear haphazard and casual.

I have found these qualities of highly organized instruction and student participation in classrooms throughout China's cities and villages. When the teacher arrives in the classroom, the students always say, "*Zao shang hao, lao shi*"—Good morning, Teacher—in unison, in elementary school, junior high school, and high school. The teacher then delivers a 40-minute lesson. There are no interruptions from misbehaving or inattentive students, no time is spent asking a student for make-up homework, and there are none of the administrative tasks that divert an American teacher's attention.

The classroom in China is for instruction and the teachers, who specialize in subject areas in both elementary and high school, have their lessons carefully planned from beginning to end. Not only do teachers map out and possibly rehearse the lesson with other teachers, but they also plan the best way to create a visual concept on the blackboard to solidify the lesson for students. Chinese teachers often add segments of the ideas to the board as they proceed, using different colored chalks to emphasize a point. By the end of the teaching period, there is a complete, visually organized display on the board. More affluent schools have computerized visual displays tied to textbooks. These too are carefully integrated into teachers' lessons.

Most American teachers' overall lesson structure is more improvised, and they seldom present the main concept or concepts visually, with the exception of some high school science and math classes or the occasional PowerPoint presentation. Although I have always planned lessons carefully, what I write on the board or display with a document camera—a word here, a sentence or illustration there—is mainly for emphasis of ideas mentioned by the class. I don't plan for a unified conceptual image to emerge. Partly this is because my lesson plans, and those of most American teachers, are open-ended and vary depending how students respond and what they contribute to the discussion.

In China, however, teachers make detailed instruction plans that they are usually able to carry to completion. Teachers in rural areas may not be as polished as those in many city schools, but their plan is still obvious, both in the ongoing lesson and on the board.

Chinese classrooms emphasize decorum, perfection, and polished performance skills. Those first lessons I'd observed in Xuzhou in 1991 were startling to me because they were so carefully choreographed and the teacher had continuous control of the classroom dialogue.

"Qian Na, read the second paragraph for us. Use a strong voice," one Xuzhou second-grade teacher told a student.

"Bai Yang, read the same paragraph. It's an important one. Read it with emotion."

"How would you feel if you couldn't find your mother?" the teacher asked, referring to a story about a lost tadpole.

Children responded: "I would be sad." "I'd be scared."

"Now," the teacher said, "read the sentence again and show how the tadpole would feel."

Everyone the teacher called on stood to speak (Chinese students always stand to speak) and read audibly and clearly. I have found this to be true not just at the demonstration "key" schools but also in regular schools. In my experience, American second-graders do not do that easily.

I have watched Chinese teachers encourage as well as pressure children to speak loudly and clearly in class, starting in first grade. "Sit down. Your voice is too soft" is a common comment. It always strikes me as harsh, but my Chinese colleagues insist that the children must learn to speak up. Several parents, however, have told me that many children are hesitant to speak up for fear of being criticized.

Chinese parents often describe how they make their kids practice to ensure their success. They help their children prepare for presentations far more actively than American parents do. Although they are as busy as U.S. parents, Chinese parents spend many more hours overseeing their children's schoolwork. Wang Yan, dean of a university program in Nanjing who was completing her Ph.D. dissertation, bought a blackboard so her daughter could show her what she learned each day in first grade, and they worked together on many homework assignments.

Wang Yan and I often met over supper to discuss these issues. She described helping her daughter, Zhang Bing, memorize lessons at home each night. For math, she would drill her on sums such as $5 + 8 = 13$, $2 + 20 = 22$, $8 + 18 = 26$. For Chinese language class, they would read and discuss stories, review the meaning and strokes of new characters, and prepare for the next day's lessons. Although her daughter was called on only occasionally in her 40-student class, she had to be ready to respond with perfect answers directly related to the text.

"They are selected to get up in front of the class sometimes to tell the news or give the weather forecast and are given a day to prepare," she said. "That gives them a chance to talk freely about something outside the textbook." When her daughter was selected to give a weather report, she and Zhang Bing searched the Internet to prepare. Rain was predicted, so they rehearsed what she would say in class. Her daughter also practiced reciting a poem, *Spring Rain*, by a famous Tang Dynasty poet that she had memorized by the time she was three years old. I asked how often Zhang Bing had a chance to speak in class. "Once so far this year," Wang Yan said. A few months later, Wang Yan sent me an email saying that her daughter had been given a second speaking assignment, as well as an opportunity to tell the class why they should elect her to lead physical education activities.

Wang Yan said preparation and practice are essential so that her daughter can perform with confidence and not bungle her limited opportunities.

In Nanjing in 2010, I watched a lanky fourth-grader, Huang Hao Ran, stand in front of the class, energy radiating in his every movement. His performance was polished and obviously practiced. He paced dramatically, then leaned forward and began to speak, his strong voice carrying to the back of the room. Having students lead small sections of the class is part of the new curriculum effort to involve them in more active learning.

"I'm Huang Hao Ran, today's student on duty. Now I will preside over the five-minute recitation." He made sure his classmates had their books open so they could read along. As if leading them in calisthenics, he said, "Ancient proverbs, ready? Go!"

"Ancient proverbs instruct you repeatedly," they read in unison. "You should read and listen to more proverbs to open your mind."

After they read several proverbs aloud, Huang Hao Ran said, "Next, I will talk about *The Romance of the Three Kingdoms*." (It is a classic novel known to most Chinese.) He struck the table in front of the class with his hand and with dramatic flare recounted a passage he had read recently. He described the scene well, including how one character, Hua Ji, tries to outwit a horse, which responds in kind. Huang Hao Ran gestured animatedly as he played both parts, ending abruptly by saying, "If you want to know what happened to Hua Ji afterwards, I'll tell you next time."

The students applauded his polished performance and the teacher stepped in, reminding the group of the activity. "Each day we have a very pleasant five-minute recitation before class. This year's materials for recitation are two books: *The Romance of the Three Kingdoms* and *A Journey to the West*. I hope more and more of you will stand on this stage to express yourself."

Chinese children also perfect their performance abilities by participating in contests run by businesses and community organizations such as newspapers, and by taking private classes—gymnastics, piano, speech, writing, calligraphy, math, and foreign languages, including English. Most families in urban areas regard these extracurricular activities and lessons as essential for gaining entrance to the best schools, which in turn positions their children to qualify for the best universities. Impressive certificates add extra clout. Official exams occur only for high school and university entrance, but at all levels tests and other means, such as certificate for extra courses, improve the possibility of being accepted. From first grade on, Chinese families urge their children to advance in these courses and earn certificates that are often packaged into well-crafted portfolios and submitted with applications to win entrance to preferred schools. It is a given in this competitive country of 1.3 billion people.

This laser focus on perfection and performance is seen even in rural areas where resources are scarce and parents have had little formal education. In An Shang, a small village on the edge of the great Locoo Plateau in central China, a group of parents talked enthusiastically about the preparation process their new principal had introduced for the local speech contest. Their school had participated in these contests before, but had ranked low. Now the children were learning to give speeches in class and gaining confidence.

"Learning to make speeches is a very important change in the school," began one parent. Others jumped in.

"The school has a speech each Monday. Every class gives one."

"My son was chosen to do it. He wrote his own speech. Then the teacher revised it. And on Monday morning, he gave the speech."

"They don't have this speech thing in other schools," one said, obviously proud of their advantage.

"Other schools say that we at An Shang School have good teachers and hard-working students ... They don't have such a good learning environment."

Parents with limited education and without similar opportunities to those in An Shang still find ways to provide their children chances though neighbors, relatives, and other means that they discover.

In the United States, expectations are quite different. Students do prepare for class presentations and rehearse for school assemblies and programs, but in my experience these are rarely honed to the perfection required of Chinese children. Arguably, part of the charm of some U.S. elementary school staged programs is their imperfect nature: the child who drops a sign; the child who makes an entrance by mistake and then runs offstage.

In U.S. classrooms, talk is informal and impromptu. There is nothing rehearsed about students' comments when the teacher asks them to come up with their own solutions and answers to questions. Teachers often break the class into small groups to discuss ideas with each other. Student comments are not expected to be perfect; they are improvised. To a Chinese observer, daily interactions in a U.S. classroom often seem haphazard. Teachers move around the room, drawing close to soft-spoken children to hear them and encourage them to talk. They are more concerned about getting all the students to participate than how accurate or polished their comments are. When students work alone at their desks or in groups, the teachers have informal conversations and discussions as needed. The recent emphasis on standardized testing has led some schools to adopt text-book driven programs that require teachers to recite publishers' lesson scripts, but students still are almost always encouraged to contribute their ideas and commentary.

During one first-grade language arts lesson that was dominated by skill training, I watched an American teacher, Ms. Henderson, explain the meaning of one vocabulary word after another in a skills-laden lesson. Yet even though this instruction was part of a highly controlled reading program, she encouraged students to express independent and spontaneously formed ideas.

She pointed to the word *gnarled*, the silent "g" making it a tough word for many first-graders. Next she showed them photos of gnarled trees, then asked what the word meant.

"I think gnarled means," one boy in a Lakers sweatshirt said, leaning forward in his desk chair. He tried again and paused. Ms. Henderson waited as he searched for the word he wanted. "Funny looking?" he said, wrinkling his nose in uncertainty.

"Right," the teacher told him as she wrote his suggestion on the board. "Can anyone add to that?"

A boy who had been rocking on his chair asked, "Does it mean they are different shapes?"

She wrote "different shapes" on the board, although it didn't quite capture the meaning, then pointed to the photos. The children offered more words: *twisted, bumpy, odd.*

A student in front piped up. "Can I bring a picture of that kind of tree?"

"Yes, good idea," the teacher said. Then returning to the words written on the board she asked, "Can anyone tell us what 'odd' means?"

A self-assured girl with an overstuffed backpack hanging from the back of her chair raised her hand. "It means like when numbers are odd or even."

The teacher laughed gently. "Well, that's a different 'odd.' That's the 'odd' we talk about in math. There are two kinds of odd." Someone else jumped in, "It's a homophone."

Building on that comment, Ms. Henderson showed them that the word is spelled the same in both uses. A homophone, she told the class, is a word that sounds the same but is spelled differently. The student had taken them slightly off-topic, but it is an important concept for them to understand so the teacher followed the thread. "Can anyone think of a homophone?"

The self-assured student's hand went up. Slowly and carefully, she said, "There's 'meet'—m-e-e-t, and then there's the kind you eat, meat—m-e-a-t. They are spelled differently and sound the same."

It was a complex idea for a first-grader to explain, and the teacher was careful to keep a couple of fidgeting students quiet until she finished. It was important to allow the girl to put her insight into her own words. How different this interaction was from the fast-moving lessons in Chinese classrooms, where there are clearly defined answers and teachers insist on perfection.

But it's not just the teachers' emphasis on their students' mastery of the lesson that makes Chinese education different. In China, the teacher's presentation of effective lessons is considered an art form. There are age-old patterns of teaching that lie deep in the culture, reinforced by daily, traditional behavior inside and outside of school. Despite governmental edicts requiring changes, highly structured, artfully crafted lessons continue to be a hallmark of Chinese education.

Changes in approach began in 2001, when the Chinese government instituted significant reforms of curriculum and teaching methods in pilot schools.[1] By 2008, I saw glimmers of change in regular school classrooms, and by 2010 a few teachers sometimes had students working in groups. They also have begun to involve students more actively in lessons. They act out skits from the book, help select answers from a classroom computer, and occasionally use demonstration materials. But overall, at least when compared with U.S. schools, Chinese teachers still maintain tight control over lesson agendas and student commentary, and the texts remain supreme.

One principal in Anhui Province told me that before the 2001 curriculum reform, the textbook was the bible for teacher and student alike.

Although the curriculum has changed, he said, the teachers and the exams have not. In fact, classroom drills and assignments remain tied to the entrance exams for high school and college. "As for the quality-oriented education called for by the central government," wrote teacher education researchers Jin Zhou of Beijing Normal University and Lynda Reed from the University of Vermont, "while school leaders, teachers, students, and parents understand its advantages, the current assessment systems for students and teachers have not changed correspondingly." This causes confusion, they said, with schools presenting a modern, interactive style to the public, while in reality using memorization-dominated methods to prepare students for exams. Zhou and Reed point out that superimposing reforms on the exam system creates a dichotomy, forcing school administrators to declare they are using modern methods while their teachers are responsible for enforcing exam-oriented teaching.[2]

In both China and the United States, teacher education varies widely from college to college and among provinces or states. In China, however, variation at the local and provincial level is overseen by the national government much more completely than in the United States where only a few nationwide requirements apply to all states. What is expected of student teachers in the two countries is also strikingly different, and it carries over into their continuing professional development.

Many American student teachers spend a full semester in classrooms. Chinese teachers spend about half that time.[3,4] Long before this, student teachers in both countries are required to observe in classrooms. Many U.S. student teachers visit weekly and become involved in class activities; Chinese student teachers go less frequently, and do not participate in classroom instruction and procedures. Rather, they watch and learn how to analyze the lessons being taught.

The experience of a recent Chinese graduate from an Anhui Province teacher education program seems typical. In her freshman year of college, she observed for only one class period. The next year, she and fellow students spent two days at a school, observing children and teachers and the methods by which different subjects are taught. In her junior year, she watched videos on how to teach specific subjects, analyzing how the demonstration teacher structured the lesson's delivery, organized materials to reinforce the lesson, and maintained a disciplined atmosphere. In the fourth and final year, she completed six weeks of teaching practice, which involved assisting a master teacher part of the time and spending many hours observing other experienced teachers.

Near the end of this final practice period, Chinese student teachers are required to give one full lesson, which is evaluated by a team that includes the college supervisor, the master teacher, and a few others from the school. Beforehand, the student teachers must plan and re-plan that lesson, getting critiques from advisors, experienced teachers, and peers, in order to perfect every aspect. Then, before teaching the lesson to a class of children, they must present it to their fellow university classmates.

Although American student teachers are required to do plenty of lesson planning and some preliminary teaching to their peers before working in the classroom, most teacher education programs stress that teaching children or adolescents in real classrooms is the best way to hone student teachers' skills and learn how to engage students in substantive, active learning. Reflection on their own experience is valued far more than analyzing the teaching methods of others.

American student teachers spend no more than a week observing a master teacher, then begin to take on one classroom responsibility after another—taking attendance, correcting and passing out papers, and helping individual students. Soon they are teaching lessons to small groups or a brief portion of a longer lesson, with the expectation they will take over almost all classroom responsibilities for at least the last week of their student teaching assignment. In elementary school that means teaching all subjects; in high school it means teaching several different classes in their area of specialization. In the college where I work, student teachers spend two sessions of about eight weeks, working full-time in different grade levels and usually in two different schools so they are exposed to various school routines. Once they have finished student teaching, they must be able to survive on their own in a classroom, usually quite isolated from any other teachers and receiving very little support or guidance.

In lengthy discussions about the differences between our systems, my colleague Yu Zhenyou, a professor of early childhood education in Beijing, has emphasized how important it is for Chinese student teachers and credentialed teachers to observe classrooms in order to learn how to improve their own teaching. Our action-oriented American system rejects the idea that observation should dominate student teaching. Fledgling teachers must try out their teaching skills right away, because in that process, with some help from their college and in-school mentors, and by reflecting on their own practice, they learn to teach. Emphasis is placed on learning to self-critique and find ways to improve in self-selected areas.

Yu has asked me more than once, incredulously, "So student teachers and employed teachers do not have a chance to go out and observe in other classes during their work day?" From his perspective and that of most Chinese educators, being critiqued and mentored by others and learning how to analyze the methods of exemplary teachers are essential. In fact this process of learning from each other is embedded in the structure of all Chinese schools, elementary and high school alike.

Coaching and critiquing are at the heart of learning to teach in China, involving frequent detailed observations and suggestions for ways to improve. This is true, not just for student teachers, but for all teachers. During the first few years of employment, Chinese teachers are considered novices. They are provided ample time to observe expert teachers and talk with them about their craft. The teaching loads of almost all urban teachers are light by U.S. standards. They teach only a few classes of the same subject and spend the rest of the day in an office shared with their teaching team grading papers, developing lesson plans, and working with students who need extra help. This is true for elementary as well as high school teachers. In China, teachers are expected to refine their art, which requires "study, practice, discussion, observation, and research," according to Lynne Paine, a researcher at Michigan State University who spent several years in China interviewing teachers, shadowing teacher candidates, and observing classes. "Teaching is seen as a complex and therefore difficult task that involves many goals to be accomplished."[5]

Teachers in China, Paine suggests, aspire to become virtuosos. Their art is teaching. Through the combination of thoroughly learning the necessary knowledge of their subject and developing a personal teaching aesthetic, they can achieve excellence. "The virtuoso teacher," she writes, "is one who has so mastered the technical knowledge of the text that she or he is able to transcend it, adding a piece of one's own self, one's own interpretation, in organizing the presentation, communicating it . . . and rendering it understandable for the audience."[6] For the most skilled, a lesson becomes an artful performance. All teachers aspire to this.

Chinese teachers, therefore, are respected for the depth of knowledge they have of their subject and for their skill in helping students understand it through questioning, recitation, and study. This requires thoughtful analysis of the subject texts and determining how to present concepts in ways that students comprehend. This is a far cry from the atmosphere U.S. teachers find themselves in, battling such prejudices as expressed in the saying, "Those who can, do, and those who can't, teach." Although parents often are appreciative of their children's and adolescents' teachers, the teaching profession is not highly regarded in the United States.

Instead of practicing lessons to performance quality or developing in-depth understanding of the details of a text, American teachers augment their lessons from the world beyond the classroom. They work to connect what they are teaching to their students' lives, to give it meaning, and to help students understand its relevance to them. And they spend time developing interesting projects to spark students' interest and imaginative engagement. In addition, they encourage students to contribute to class discussions and ask questions. U.S. teachers also enrich lessons with materials they bring into the classroom from the real world—from frogs and autumn leaves to guest speakers and additional books related to a topic of study. Chinese teachers do not bring in additional materials. In all the Chinese classrooms I have observed over a period of 20 years, I have seen only one apple and a few vegetables used to supplement the instruction, and this was in a small village school. There are now extra homework booklets that reproduce parts of the texts with slightly different questions than those the teacher used, but parents say that although schools use these to get students thinking independently, they are quite limited. When these booklets ask students for supplementary information, only citations from the Internet or encyclopedias are wanted, not students' original ideas.

Nor do Chinese teachers interact extensively with groups of students or work to keep them contributing to a class discussion or activity, the way U.S. teachers do. In some Chinese schools that are implementing the new curriculum, especially those with smaller class sizes, teachers do go from group to group, checking on what students are learning, but there is virtually no interaction with individual students. The Chinese teacher works with the whole group, and group activities are highly controlled by the teacher.

Scholarship, or *xuewen*, "makes [teachers] proud of themselves and respected by students and colleagues," says Liping Ma, a math teacher from China. "They are supposed to know much more than what they have to teach." She cites a popular adage, "If you want to give students a cup of water, you have to have one bucket for yourself."[7] Young Chinese adults, though frustrated by the pedantic and straightjacket nature of education they have received, say they have high regard for such teachers because they display a depth of subject matter knowledge. "They weren't very creative at all, or provocative," Fan Hao, a young university instructor, said of many of her best teachers. "But they had a very solid grounding in their fields of knowledge, and I'm grateful for having had them as teachers. They weren't exciting, but I respected them a lot."[8]

This respect for a teacher's knowledge goes back millennia. One of the strongest traditions—having students memorize and explicate texts—harkens back to the last millennium when those who scored too low on the imperial exams to join government officialdom became teachers. Memorization and repetition were all they knew.[9] Lynne Paine, the researcher from Michigan, says, "Chinese teachers see themselves, for the most part, as transmitters of knowledge or, for those more progressive teachers, as helping students actively engage with knowledge." But that knowledge must be mastered from texts.[10] In ancient days, they were Confucian texts; today they are the current textbooks used to prepare students for exams.

A student's spontaneous comments are not tolerated in class. As one young parent I interviewed said, "In class, if my junior high school son expresses his opinions, the teachers will get mad. If he answers on his tests with his own opinion, he will get a zero. He offers his opinions at home."[11] In contrast, most U.S. students understand that their opinions and questions are usually welcome in their classes. Although many American educators would like to see much more open-ended inquiry and use of critical thinking, the Chinese already covet the amount that now exists in U.S. classrooms.

Another fundamental aspect of teacher education in China is collaboration, which continues throughout teachers' lives and strengthens both their knowledge base and their skills. This is so different from the American approach to teaching that it has taken me some time to comprehend that all Chinese teachers regard themselves as part of a team that collaborates regularly, observes each others' lessons often, and analyzes their effectiveness. What begins with the student-teaching experience and extends into a teacher's novice years, then continues as a never-ending process of collaborative support throughout their professional life. American teachers are provided almost no such support.

Central to this lifetime of collaboration for Chinese teachers are the *jiaoyanzu*, teaching research groups within each school that meet weekly on a formal basis and casually throughout the school day. Organized by grade level and/or subject area, these small groups of teachers prepare lessons together, discuss curriculum challenges, and critique each other's teaching. They often share an office, so they have both formal and informal interchanges to foster collegiality and coach one another. This process helps them polish lessons to perfection. It is common to mix old, middle-aged, and young teachers in each group to encourage "the old to bring along the young" (*lao dai qing*)[12] This arrangement enables teachers to deepen the lessons and students' understanding of specific content. Some Chinese educators, however, feel that this process hinders change because it perpetuates the notion that the older, more traditional teachers are experts to whom newer teachers must defer. When young teachers consider bringing new methods they have learned in their university courses into the classroom, they are often encouraged to replace them with the more traditional ones valued by older teachers. "This can lead to conformity," Yu Zhenyou said, "rather than change." Regardless of such pitfalls, the *jiaoyanzu* provides all Chinese teachers with a support community that respects their professional abilities. Sporadic attempts have been made in the United States to create mentoring programs for novice and experienced teachers, but these come and go with the ebb and flow of budgets and with administrators' beliefs in their importance. Mentoring is not a part of the American teacher development culture.

Forward-looking Chinese administrators are using these *jiaoyanzu* to implement national curriculum directives for change. The teachers and administrators at one of the schools I have visited several times had been working for two years to develop a better curriculum and make long-range changes in their teaching methods. Zhu Yan Qin, the school principal and Communist Party secretary, said they do this by having teachers attend district or area meetings where they hear experts and discuss new ideas. Then the school's executive staff and head teachers work to implement the experts' ideas, within their school. Zhu Yan Qin emphasized the importance, especially for the young teachers, of how the ongoing collaboration groups help facilitate this process. "They could not learn to teach or to improve their teaching without these groups," she said. She could not understand how American teachers can be expected to prepare lessons if they are not given time to meet together at school on a regular basis. Sometimes her teachers meet by grade level, at other times by subjects. They decide on one topic or area they want to work on. They observe one of the strongest group members, called "backbone teachers," give a demonstration lesson and then meet to discuss it. The teacher who taught the lesson explains why she or he did certain things and the observers give suggestions. Finally, they talk about how they all can improve the lesson or method of delivery, and then use the model in their own classes.

American teachers, in general, are not accustomed to substantial collaboration. Traditionally elementary school teachers have worked in isolation. One elementary teacher said her school had offered demonstration lessons at one point. The observing teachers were asked to state three positive things they saw and one "wish" about what else they would like to see. But she said most observers only mentioned the positive things they saw because they hesitated to criticize a colleague. Another teacher said she felt supported by the teaching staff of her school, but it was based on a hands-off mutual respect and assumed that they all knew what they were doing. In U.S. high schools teachers often have randomly assigned preparation periods that can lead to occasional informal collaborative efforts among a few teachers, but purposeful peer mentoring is seldom an on-going process.

A number of U.S. elementary schools now have grade-level teams meet one hour a week, usually during recesses or by using various support staff to cover their classes. Sometimes these groups work with a literacy coach on curriculum issues or they may deal with particular problems that need solving. But fine-tuning or critiquing lessons is not included. Some U.S. junior and senior high schools have about an hour a week of common planning time. This is a move in the right direction, but needs to be considered much more seriously. Most U.S. schools do not have the staff and flexibility to arrange such collaboration to the extent found in Chinese schools.

In sum, having observed the spectrum of teaching in China, I have come to realize that American teachers have no idea how improvisational and unstructured their classrooms are and the positive effect this has on student thinking. Where U.S. lessons are open-ended, impromptu, and encourage spontaneous and imperfect student participation, Chinese lessons are preplanned, often well-rehearsed, and require students to respond from texts they have studied thoroughly and usually memorized. In addition, Chinese teachers have no idea that their in-depth collaborative and peer-critiquing is a unique advantage. These different practices are deeply embedded in the histories and teaching cultures of each country. It would be helpful for the teachers, administrators, and policy makers of each country to understand in some depth what the other country is doing, what each believes is the benefit as well as pitfalls of its practices, and how they can be improved. In doing so, it is important to keep in mind that the twenty-first century demands that students learn to think on their feet and solve ever-changing problems in collaborative teams with well-informed solutions.

10

Aiming toward College

Taped on a wall at my desk is a newspaper photograph of people throning a school building in an unnamed Chinese city where thousands of students are taking the national exam for college admission. Some are holding signs urging on their children and grandchildren. Others are praying, eyes shut, hands clasped in front of their faces. Others stare into the distance, worry etched in their face. The anxiety is palpable, and it is all because of the exam, which is administered in local schools across China on the same two days of June. During these two days, traffic is re-routed and construction projects are halted as parents, grandparents, aunts, and uncles stand watch, some never leaving until their loved one emerges.

One exam taker I interviewed from Jiangsu Province, whose parents stood outside the exam hall both days, said it helped to have them standing vigil. "When I have done well, my father is happy," she said. "When I don't do well and he is not happy, then I try harder. So knowing he was out there helped me try my very best. It encouraged me." Another, from Beijing, said her parents were there and were more worried about the test than she was. The photo and comments of recent exam takers remind me of the legions of parents I have met over my years of research in China whose lives are devoted to their only child's success. That success hinges on the score the high school graduates receive on the June exam. The stakes are high as the graduates chase limited slots in the top universities that many families deem essential for providing their child access to financially viable jobs in the future.

There is an all-or-nothing quality to the Chinese quest for college. Chinese parents rely on children's financial support in their retirement years. Therefore parents and children alike aim high. In the United States, the college entrance process causes parents and students plenty of anxiety, to be sure, especially in the final frenzy of meeting application deadlines. But that is nowhere near the level of stress I've seen in China, because U.S. students have multiple avenues to excel and these are spread over time. First of all, American students have eight semesters in high school to amass a good grade-point average. They can take a preliminary scholastic test to prepare them for the actual SAT (Scholastic Aptitude Test) or ACT college admission exams, which they can retake to try to boost their scores. Colleges also consider an applicant's participation in a variety of sports, leadership, and volunteer activities that display character, athletic skills, and other values prized by admissions officers. U.S. families face an ever-increasing financial burden to give their children a chance at a good career, but the stress is different from what is found in China, where there isn't an equivalent, vast network of state and community colleges that provides access to what families consider substantial professions. Although in China and the United States, test scores, activities, which colleges to apply to, and the increasing financial burden all affect families, the level of stress is significantly different. In both countries, parents of college-bound students become immersed in their children's academic preparations and often get caught up by what other parents are doing. Are they alert to activities that could give their child a competitive edge? Will this look better on their records than that? How should they prepare their child for the exams, by hiring tutors or enrolling them in an intensive course? The bottom line: Parents everywhere want to provide the very best opportunities for their children's future success.

In China, I talked with a number of freshmen who had been admitted to a top university in Jiangsu Province. In one group of three, two young women were from the well-off areas of Beijing and Jiangsu provinces, and a young man was from a city in the western province of Sichuan. I had heard plenty about the *gaokao,* the college entrance exam that students spend years preparing for, and I wanted to hear about the experience from those who had just run the final gauntlet.

Lily, a confident Beijing student, said the exam wasn't that difficult for her "because I am a Beijing student from a good high school. The pressure was not as much for us as it is for students in other places. Before we took the entrance exam we did a lot of practice. So, when I took the real exam I didn't feel nervous. It was just like the rest of our tests."

I was surprised at her calm attitude, but kept quiet. Lily said that during her last year of high school they prepared in a variety of ways that were not as boring as exam exercises. "The teachers thought up things to entertain us."

Rose, who came from the wealthy eastern province of Jiangsu, was eager to describe her unique experience. "I think our school is different from those in many other cities," she said. "It is intended to develop all-round students, and we had a lot of activities, even when we studied for the exam our last year. We had different types of lectures and went to a needy community to do volunteer work for the people. We even watched films."

"So that's very different from other schools?" I asked.

She nodded energetically and pointed to Lily. "We two are from key schools." These are the schools that receive extra government funds and often are used to test new curriculum.

The young man, Chen, looked glum. Although he was from a major city in Sichuan, school resources in the south-central China province are much fewer than in Jiangsu and Beijing. "All we had was just papers and books," he said. "Before the examination, I didn't watch TV or films for three years. In fact, most of my classmates and friends had not watched TV or played computer games. So by our last year of high school we were all crazy. We did nothing but study for the exam. In our last year, the school had lectures about stress from psychologists, but I only had a chance to hear one for thirty minutes. My parents were worried about my depression."

"You did paper and pencil work for three years to prepare for the exam?" I asked, to make sure I'd heard him correctly.

Lily, the Beijing student, interrupted with an urgency belying her earlier nonchalance. Her finger jabbing the air to the staccato rhythm of her words, she declared, "For *twelve* years, for *twelve* years we were preparing for the exam. When we were going to primary school, our parents were educating us about how to pass the entrance exam. If you want to enter college, you have to be better than anyone else on exams. The only access to college is the entrance exam and so we are always doing everything for it, from the very beginning of our school years. From first grade on." The exam may have been easier for Lily and her preparation not as harrowing, but she clearly had experienced enormous angst.

I talked with freshmen from other high schools, including some who had failed the June exam and were attending either three-year private colleges at enormous expense to their extended families or three-year specialty public colleges with low rankings. Their stories were very much the same. Those who went to elite schools found that the last year of study—which is incomparable in its intensity to anything experienced by American students—included an occasional interesting activity. Students at other Chinese high schools did nothing but pencil-and-paper exercises day in and day out, memorizing text after text. All high schools conducted practice tests throughout the year to get the students used to the form and the need for pressured concentration, and most students were required to return to school after dinner as well as on weekends to study. Students from rural areas who attended consolidated boarding schools were not allowed to go home or have visitors for the last three months before the June exam.

Ruizhe Wang,[1] a graduate student from a prestigious Beijing university, said they studied from 8 A.M. to 10 P.M. or midnight every day, seven days a week throughout his entire senior year of high school. "It was very repetitive. Our main aim was to enhance our proficiency in answering questions." He needed to improve his accuracy in Chinese, English, mathematics, and science, which included chemistry, biology, and physics. As a math and science major, Wang took an exam that emphasized those subjects. Humanities majors take a different test that has more Chinese and English, less math, and includes sections on history, geography, and political science, although these last three vary in different provinces.

A freshman from the coastal province of Fujian who had been admitted to a prestigious university said she had spent her entire childhood studying for the exam. In her province, the exam was not as difficult as in some other places, she said. But when she got to the university, she discovered that she was behind other students academically. "I am finding my high school education was not so good," she said ruefully. She had to work much harder at university than those from better urban schools.

Ruizhe Wang explained that this is a problem in China, especially in the schools outside of major cities. Most focus only on preparing students to deal with the exam. "Their education is completely test based, so the students may not know anything apart from the test content," said Wang. "I think it's better in cities like Beijing, where I went to school, and other major cities where we learned some material beyond the exam topics."

In China as in the United States, children whose parents have a fair amount of education and are school savvy seem to have an easier time gaining access to college than do those from less privileged backgrounds. U.S. high school students from families with little academic knowledge and from large schools with few college advisors struggle to learn what courses they need to take to gain admission, the quality of work they must produce, and the many other requirements that must be met.

The Chinese news media often report on extreme cases of parents who force excessive test preparation regimens on their children. The

40 or so college students I have interviewed described varying levels of parental involvement. Some reported feeling pressured from the beginning of elementary school. Others said their parents made sure they were doing their work, but also understood how much stress they were under. However, if their work fell short in some way, no matter how understanding their parents were, the students said they were told that they needed to work harder. Even a Chinese family that planned to emigrate to Canada, so their 12-year-old son could avoid the pressure-cooker of high school, made sure that while he still attended Chinese schools, he completed four hours of homework a night and at least a day-and-a-half of work on weekends. A successful professional woman, Wang Wenyu, described how her kindly father had charted her test scores and those of her friends in junior high school because she began falling behind. He continued until she became the highest ranking student.

The Sichuan student, Chen, summed up the general sentiment about the path to college. "There is pressure from all around, I can't describe it," he said. "If you are a *good* student, you must get a high score on the exam and you must go to a famous university to prove yourself. The pressure is there every day, everywhere—at school, at home, and in the general culture of the country."

In China, students and parents are focused on getting into one of only about ten top universities if they want good-paying jobs in substantial businesses or government positions. It seems rather like the race to get into the eight Ivy League colleges and a few other highly rated U.S. universities. But the magnitude of difference is staggering: Each year, close to ten million Chinese high school graduates take the *gaokao*, and a significant number aim for seats at those ten prestigious institutions compared with less than two million U.S. graduating seniors seeking placement at about 3,800 accredited institutions.[2]

Over the last two decades, the Chinese government has pushed to expand the number of colleges and universities. The Ministry of Education reports that 57 percent of the high school graduates taking the college entrance exam in 2008 were accepted to colleges, and 72 percent would enroll in 2011.[3] This is an astronomical increase from the early 1990s, when popular estimates put the percent of high school graduates admitted to colleges at 5 percent. However, parents, especially urban middle-class parents, consider the majority of those colleges inferior. Many insist adamantly that the only way their children will be able to support their families is by gaining entrance to one of the top universities or find an alternate route, such as an overseas education.

Yunmei, a friend since my first trip to China, has explained the Chinese college system to me better than anyone else. She knows it inside and out. She taught at Nanjing University for several decades until her retirement, and she has had two children go through university. Her daughter teaches at a university that specializes in distant learning, and together they have written a textbook for junior college-level courses. Yunmei has taught adult night classes and she has friends who teach at a private college attached to a good university.

After the ten or so top tier colleges, such as Tsinghua, Beijing, Fudan, and Nanjing Universities, come the universities for teachers, the technological universities, and a host of others. Below these are the semiprivate universities, which are associated with the prestige universities but cost considerably more. Jinling College, for instance, is associated with Nanjing University and benefits from its highly rated parent school, whose faculty often teach at the college to earn extra money. Below the semiprivate institutions are the junior colleges and technical universities, some run by government departments, such as the railways, that Yunmei said are more like U.S. community colleges. Finally, there are purely private colleges.

The private/public universities, or at least Jinling and the one her granddaughter attends, have two programs: a four-year program that grants the equivalent of a bachelor of arts and a three-year program that is more job oriented and does not grant a degree. Many private colleges, including the renowned Xi'an Translators' University, are not allowed to grant bachelors degrees. Their graduates must take a national exam to obtain one.

Although Chinese parents actively investigate colleges and how to gain entrance to them, it is the high school teachers who make the final decisions about what university or subject to apply to for most students, because they have the most information about colleges and also about student strengths. Most select their colleges after taking the exam, then apply to a few universities that will consider them based on the score they earned. But within those universities, they also must apply to several departments in order of choice. Departments are rated differently. A given social work department may be ranked much lower in national ratings than the same university's history department. Ruizhe Wang selected a top university as his first choice, but he was accepted into his second choice department there. Many Chinese students and their parents choose an uninspiring department and a potentially unemployable major at a prestigious college, rather than a preferred major at a less highly rated college because they believe their job prospects are improved by attending the higher-ranked university.

The U.S. college admissions process has its own pitfalls and stresses. My husband and I recently received an email from a friend.

"The college application, acceptance, and rejection season is done at our house," wrote Judy Hurlbut, an energetic mother who lives in Alaska with her one daughter. "THANK GOODNESS!!! What an awful time."[4]

A year earlier Hurlbut had written, "Jessica and I are in the throes of college applications. It might be more accurate to say I am in the throes! She has been somewhat engaged and I sense from all her friends who were here for a birthday sleepover two weeks ago that all of the kids are feeling tense and confused—and some are more overwhelmed than others."

In a long phone conversation after the email announcing the end of the acceptance–rejection phase, Hurlbut said they were still coping with how to pay for Jessica's education. As an educator who has worked within many schools and with social service agencies, Hurlbut is savvy about how college admission works, yet she still found the process stressful, frustrating, and many parts of it puzzling. Friends without as much knowledge about how to negotiate the various aspects of their children's college admissions preparations were even more stressed, missed important deadlines, or just gave up and had their children apply only to the local state university where the odds of admission were greater. Students who did not get into a four-year state college said they would attend a local community college for a year or two and figure it out from there.

Unlike China the college entry race does not really begin until the third year of high school in the United States. Many parents do some preliminary investigating of colleges and prod their children earlier, but they focus on other activities and interests as well.

Americans know that their children can get a quality education at many colleges besides the most competitive schools. While they may not develop the contacts to be on a fast track in a Fortune 500 company, or join an elite law firm right out of law school, they still can aspire to substantial and satisfying jobs.

During the earlier school years, most U.S. families of college-bound students engage in a low-key effort to explore college options. Parents may begin by scanning websites and tucking college visits into family vacations whenever feasible to give their children a feel for the atmosphere of different campuses. They may talk with admissions officers and attend a lecture or two, as well as try to get a sense of what interests their children.

For American parents who have not attended college, there are public school programs such as College Bound Dreams[5] to help parents and children understand what courses are required for college entrance and the study habits needed to succeed in those courses. Elementary school teachers generally encourage children to think about college so that they begin to believe it is a possibility. By high school, students for the most part have been sorted into those going to college and those who are not, and the courses are different.

Most American children also are exposed to a host of extracurricular activities, such as swimming, basketball, art and music programs, and summer camps, that are aimed at providing children with a well-rounded life experience, to let them have fun and keep them involved. Even academic summer schools for students who need or want extra work are designed with a variety of enjoyable activities to create an upbeat atmosphere. Summer and after-school programs, so necessary for working parents, are usually selected for the balance of fun, learning, and safety that parents want for their children. Chinese parents seek much the same outlets for their children, but with less emphasis on fun and balance. American parents are often trying to expose their kids to new experiences, ones they will enjoy as they learn to cooperate with others, and explore various interests. U.S. parents appear to be less concerned than Chinese parents about their children developing specific skills in these settings.

Many American youngsters also learn to be self-sufficient, often from an early age. They are taught to clean their rooms, help with household chores, maybe even cook, and care for younger siblings or neighbors' children. They mow lawns, fix people's computers, or do errands for pay. They are encouraged to make decisions along the way and are expected to develop more independence at a much earlier age than most Chinese children. In high school, and often earlier, many American teenagers are active in clubs, in sports and community service, and church groups. Many schools require community service in order to graduate. By high school, they also are likely to hold part-time jobs or internships that help them to learn skills and responsibility as well as contribute to their living expenses and savings for college.

A number of American families start college funds when their children are in preschool in the hope that these savings will defray some of the college expenses. However, most students need scholarships, grants, and loans to pay the large fees.

In China, sending children to university is a financial sacrifice for all low- and middle-income families, and it is not uncommon for all the relatives to contribute to one child's college education. Because of changing government support structures in China, public universities that used to be free now cost around 6,000 *yuan* a year for tuition and housing[6] (about $940) in 2011, and private colleges are many times more expensive even though they do not offer degrees. (The average family income in China was about $2,000 in 2006.[7]) Urban middle-class families earn much more than this. However, as a percentage of income, U.S. private colleges are far more costly. Princeton University, one of the Ivy League institutions on the east coast, and the University of the Pacific on the west coast both cost about $53,000 a year, including tuition, meals, housing, and fees in 2011. Public universities are relatively cheaper but they are still expensive. The cost to attend University of California campuses at Los Angeles and Berkeley, both research universities, in 2012 is pegged at about $30,000 for California residents and is projected to rise further. The state universities of New York and Arizona are projected at about $19,000 and $22,000 respectively for state residents, and the University of North Carolina at $28,000. Fees at state universities for out-of-state residents are equal to private colleges. Students attending college often struggle to make ends meet.[8]

All these threads come together by the junior year of high school in households across the United States as college-bound students become completely immersed in the application process. The options are daunting. Where will they get in? How will it be paid for? Will government loans continue to be available? What can they do to qualify for scholarships? Athletic excellence? High grade-point averages? Special interests and projects?

Once they begin looking at specific colleges—there are about 3,800 accredited four-year colleges in the United States[9]—students are also weighing what they may major in and where their strengths and interests lie. These are pretty vague for most American teenagers. Even those who feel certain about their career goals are likely to change their mind in the first year of college, and, in fact, most colleges do not require students to decide on a major until the end of their sophomore year. In contrast, college-bound students in China must select their general major—science or humanities—midway through high school in order to prepare for the right exam. Once they are accepted to a college department, they take almost all courses within that department whether or not they like it. Changing departments and fields is extremely difficult.

American parents without a college background rely on secondary resources—friends, relatives, and neighbors who have attended college, college counselors, who are increasingly scarce as budget cuts eliminate them, and high school teachers willing to spend extra time advising. There is also the Internet. But for a parent or student who does not have some understanding of what information is important, websites can be overwhelming. Chinese parents without college—and for many, without high school—education rely heavily on similar resources, and they face the same hurdles.

In the United States, the independent College Board offers substantial information, much of it accessible on the Internet. Although that information is tailored toward the college entrance tests it sells, the College Board does offer parents and students links to scholarship information and primers on choosing, preparing, and paying for college. There also are multiple links within categories, all supplying a myriad of other links: How to create a list of possible colleges; what criteria should be used to narrow the list. (The applicants are advised to narrow their choice to ten or fewer colleges.) A separate stream explains how to navigate the various parts of college applications and how to write a compelling essay.

Rankings by organizations and magazines, such as *U.S. News & World Report,* offer comparisons that can help narrow the selection criteria: large versus small institutions, public or private colleges, the most prestigious or the least, and how far from home. Then there are the Ivy League universities, eight of the nation's most venerable colleges, which are among the most difficult to get into, not least because of their reputation for providing students with a path to join the nation's elite. A freshman at a well-known science institute (though not part of the Ivy League, but rated in the top ten institutions nationally by *US News 2011*) told me that some of his friends had set their sights on a specific prestigious university and were crushed when they were not accepted. He felt that was unwise and applied to ten different schools, including a sure-bet state university along with several prestigious universities. He said he would have been satisfied going to most of them even though he had a few favorites. He and many other U.S. students look for challenging course work, a dynamic college community that provides access to experiences beyond the classroom, fieldwork, laboratory research with professors, study abroad, service work in communities, and interning in corporations and associations related to their interests. Those are available at many U.S. colleges and universities. They help the students expand their perspectives and let them know what is available that is new to them.

In China, a student's future turns on a single exam score and a small set of college options. Most U.S. colleges have multiple criteria for admissions—from college entrance test scores to leadership potential to ability to take initiative. Here's what the website of the University of California at Los Angeles says their admissions officers are looking for besides the standard high school courses and respectable college exam scores:

> **Personal qualities of the applicant,** including leadership ability, character, motivation, tenacity, initiative, originality, creativity, intellectual independence, responsibility, insight, maturity, and demonstrated concern for others and for the community. These qualities may not be reflected in traditional measures of academic achievement. They may be found elsewhere in the application and judged by the reader as positive indicators of the student's ability to succeed at UCLA and beyond.[10]

This leaves American parents and their children mired in a guessing game with few clues as to why applicants are accepted to some colleges and not others.

Scores on the SAT or ACT general college entrance exams are fundamental to most applications, to be sure, although students can take the exam multiple times to better their scores. But the rest of the application components carry significant weight—the essays, the lists of extracurricular activities, community service, and personal references. Often the best guidance to entry requirements for many colleges is the profile of the last incoming class when it is provided. For instance, Amherst College in Massachusetts gives the breakdown on its website of the incoming freshmen in September 2011[11] by gender, percentage of students of color, those in the top 10 percent of their high school class, number of valedictorians, the number of applicants versus the number accepted, and more. Amherst, like many others, also gives the mean college entrance exam scores of its recent incoming class, which for the SAT was about 1500 for the combined critical reading and math sections (1600 is a perfect score). Then they give the range that includes students with scores several hundred points lower. From these kinds of data, it is almost impossible for applicants to predict whether they have a shot at a particular college.

Assembling the various elements of a college application is a challenge in the United States. Students must send high school transcripts and test scores, find people to write recommendation letters and ensure they are delivered, and write a compelling description of their accomplishments and extracurricular activities. Finally, students must write at least one essay or personal statement, and often several for colleges that have different requirements.

In China, the goal from the earliest grades is mastering the information on the national test. In the United States, the focus is on developing many talents. Do well in school, yes, and from the beginning, if you want to go to college. But there is much more leeway in American schools, many different ways to succeed, to interact with teachers and to ask questions, and to be engaged in learning. The college-bound student is building a resume, not just of academic work, but also of other endeavors to attract attention. If a high school student launches a small business or composes songs, that is likely to be noticed by colleges.

A freshman at an elite scientific institute with a small undergraduate program told me that he is sure his high school research projects helped him gain admission. His SAT scores, he said, were not very good compared with the school's very high student average, but while in high school he had been accepted into a summer research project at a large company. Working in a team with a college student and a graduate student, he helped develop software for a biotech project. A mentor guided them, but they were expected to develop usable software. He said it was the most valuable summer of his life: Before he'd graduated from high school he learned to conduct professional research and collaborate with a very diverse group of individuals on a common goal. In junior high school, he and other students organized walk-a-thons and other activities to raise money for poverty-stricken children in India. He continued to lead that project through his senior year, something an admissions officer could not help but notice.

Several U.S. students I have interviewed applied to about a dozen colleges, each with different requirements. Even those colleges with a common application have their own additional requirements—different due dates, extra essays to write, and emphases on different achievements. Judy Hurlbut said it was a challenge for her daughter to keep track of everything, especially when she was also taking demanding courses, running track, and doing other projects. Hurlbut finally made a spreadsheet to keep track of the requirements for all the potential colleges.

The transition from high school to college is not easy for many students, but it seems to be more challenging for Chinese students than for Americans. U.S. students tend to view college as a means for expanding their horizons, of developing their individual interests and talents, and for learning marketable skills. They are anxious to stretch their intellect and understanding of big ideas or dig deeper into topics. They usually begin with a smorgasbord of courses so they can probe different fields and gradually narrow them to a major. The freedom they experience—of being adults—can take time to manage, and balancing academics with social life does not always come easily.

The lifestyle shift between high school and college is far greater in China because American students have been balancing academics and other school activities—clubs, athletics, band, student council—with jobs, community volunteering, church, and sports leagues for years.

Many Chinese students view college in reverse. Beginning in first grade, a student has been primed and pushed to score high on the national college entrance exam, and when they reach college they want to relax. A young faculty member in a large university near the east coast of China said high school teachers tell students again and again that once they pass the exam and get into a good college, they will not have to work so hard again. But once they are in college, they do have to work. He said students are frustrated by this. Chinese students also find their sudden independence unsettling. An upper classman at one university told me that it was difficult to learn to manage time by themselves, because "all the way through school, and especially in high school, every minute was managed for us."

The Sichuan student, Chen, described it well. "In China, when we were in primary school our parents always told us that 'only study can change your fate.' But now I am in university, and I still don't know how to change my fate by studying." He was glad he had made it to one of the prestigious universities, but he was frustrated that his way forward was not clear, especially since graduates he knew who had studied hard were having a terrible time getting jobs partly because of the global recession but also because universities were turning out more graduates in his field (English) than were needed.

A freshman from Henan Province, inland from Shanghai about 500 miles, said he had been preparing for the college entrance exam all his life but had no idea how to proceed now that he'd reached his goal. "I think that the pressure in university is more stressful," he said. "We have to decide which activities we should take part in. It's all about our own deciding; but I haven't had this kind of experience and I can't make the best use of my time. So I just waste time."

Many, if not most, American college students also need to learn to organize their time and studies effectively, but they have had much more experience doing so by the time they finish high school than their Chinese counterparts.

Imaginative Engagement

Chinese educators and parents alike complain that their children are rarely encouraged to use their imagination or develop their creative talents. Xu Lei, a linguistics instructor, still recalls the day her second-grade sports program was rained out, the teacher told stories to pass the time and asked the children to share. She enthusiastically raised her hand. The teacher asked what story she wanted to tell. When Xu Lei said it was one she had made up, the teacher replied sharply, "No. You can't tell that type of story. It needs to be one we know."

"I still remember my frustration and humiliation," said Xu Lei, the mother of a two-year-old and a visiting scholar at my college. "It's a vivid memory after 25 years. Children in China are squelched early."

I have heard many similar tales from Chinese friends and colleagues, which makes it tempting to set up an either/or dichotomy—that American classrooms are filled with imaginative engagement and Chinese schools trample all attempts at creativity. But education—like life—is more complex. In the United States, talk about innovation is common, and students generally have more opportunity to express their ideas and actively contribute to class activities than Chinese children do. Yet American students are often assigned unimaginative worksheets and mundane questions at the end of textbook chapters and critical-thinking or innovative problem-solving lessons are omitted. It is also incorrect to say that the Chinese education system completely stifles creative impulses. Although many Chinese parents say that independent thinking has to be developed at home because schools focus entirely on exam results, I have seen classroom instruction loosen up over the last 20 years, at least in the elementary grades. In addition, some urban schools are offering an increasing variety of art and music lessons. Although these arts courses are often focused on learning technique, they do allow students some self-expression.

Based on my experience as a teacher and a researcher, I believe both countries would benefit from much more substantive imaginative engagement with academic material. When students are engaged, you can see it in their eyes, in the eager tilt of their bodies. That energy is missing when they are bored witless.

You can see the excitement when students connect a story's ideas or a person's experiences to their own lives, or when a math teacher challenges students to find their new desk assignments using an x/y grid map. Significant learning is taking place when a student struggles through draft after draft of an essay, then shares it with the class, or when a group plans and brings to fruition a project to educate fellow students about diabetes after researching everything about the disease. You can see students' enthusiastic engagement when they realize how to light a bulb with batteries and wire and what happens when they change the variables. This does not mean students need to be entertained or heaped with praise, although enjoyment does help stimulate and reinforce learning. But they should be encouraged to use all their abilities and knowledge and to be challenged to accomplish even more. Soviet psychologist Lev Vygotsky (1896–1934) theorized that students' conceptual development advances significantly when learning environments challenge them and show them new possibilities.[1] I have seen this kind of engagement take place in American classrooms and in a few Chinese classrooms that promote active student involvement. But such opportunities are diminishing in the United States because of laws requiring improved student performance as measured by standardized tests and they do not exist in most Chinese schools.

Chinese teachers and parents I have encountered over the years regularly ask me how they can introduce more creativity into their children's academic lives. They are more than frustrated by the traditionally narrow Chinese curriculum and the dominance of the exam system. Even Li Jianhua, principal of an elite Beijing high school with a reputation for academic excellence and innovation, makes a distinction between high test scores and the mastery required for transformative knowledge. Though his students' math and science scores are lauded by Westerners, he believes their education is insufficient. "On the surface, Chinese students can get very high scores in math and science," Li Jianhua told *Education Week* reporter Sean Cavanagh. "But they don't really grasp the true meaning of math and science." He added that "science and math are analytical tools ... to explore the world. People in China see math and science as a tool to change their destiny, not to explore the world."[2] Instead of building gadgets, Li Jianhua said, China's math and science graduates should be doing research to understand nature or human phenomena. This, in his opinion, would foster valuable imaginative engagement that the current emphasis on rote memorization for testing cannot.

A teenager from southern China, who was an exchange student at a public high school northwest of Atlanta, told Cavanaugh that although her U.S. classmates' math and science skills weren't equal to those of her friends in China, her American classmates had more freedom to take elective classes and they learned to become leaders. They were not afraid to ask questions or give a wrong answer, unlike students in China. "They really enjoyed learning."[3]

During my most recent observations in American classrooms, I was struck by the difference between them and the most flexible ones I'd seen in China. Even at the most conventional U.S. schools, the difference is notable. In spite of the heavy emphasis on testing, interactions between students and teacher are generally more casual and aimed at pushing students to stretch their thinking than anything in Chinese schools. In a downtown Los Angeles neighborhood, I observed a teacher who created a rich learning environment for her third-graders by weaving serious skill-building into engaging projects. Following a scripted program, but given latitude in using it by her principal, Mary Norris involved the children in a discussion in preparation for reading their assignment about how money systems evolved in North America. The fictional piece told of some of the disputes and misunderstandings that occurred before a regular monetary system was developed. The children had spent time paging through the story looking at pictures, skimming for unfamiliar words, and getting an overall view of what the narrative was about. Norris then invited them to ask questions about the story, what the reading program calls "Wonderings."

"Where do you find gold?" one boy asked.

"Do you know the answer to that?" Norris asked the class. When some students said gold comes from the ground and from rocks, she responded, "If you can answer the question you are asking, then it really isn't something you are wondering about."

Another student, referring to characters in the story, asked, "Why were people fighting?" Norris said they would need to answer that question through their reading or investigate it in other ways, and it was certainly something to wonder about. Encouraged, others began contributing questions:

"Why are Americans different now from a long time ago?"

"Why did people use shells instead of money like us?"

"Why did money develop from metal?" Some began to exchange ideas with their neighbors while others raised their hands to make suggestions to the whole class.

Norris let them share on the side, which gave children who were less sure of themselves a chance to express ideas. By the end of the short lesson, fully a third of the students had contributed their ideas. The teacher wrote a few of the most open-ended ones on sentence strips that she posted on the bulletin board to be answered while reading the story over the next few days.

This method of making multiple connections to reinforce learning was a revelation to my colleague Yang Dongyan's son, who spent his sophomore year at a high school in Michigan while his parents were exchange teachers. The teenager loved his physics class because he had to apply theories he was learning to actual experiments. Two years after returning to China he continued to be amazed at the excitement he had felt. Not only were scientific theories connected to reality, in other classes he could choose projects from a variety of topics, find information from many sources, and assess their accuracy. What's more, teachers encouraged him to develop his own views about topics. He gained greater and more lasting knowledge from this type of learning, he said, than he did when he memorized texts as required in China.

U.S. educators would do well to avoid fostering those same repetitive learning methods in a headlong rush to boost standardized test scores. I've seen the perils of demanding that teachers use highly controlled curriculum and concentrated test preparations.

Recently, I visited a teacher at a school in eastern Los Angeles, whose first-grade classes I'd observed over the years. She had always successfully engaged her students' imaginations while developing their skills and academic strengths. Now, saddled with a scripted language arts program that her school administrators required teachers to follow to the letter, she struggled to keep the children interested. She began the day with an hour-long math lesson that was half lecture, albeit with some student participation, and half exercises applying what she had taught. This was followed immediately by a two-hour language arts lesson, broken only by a brief recess, nearly all of it devoted to skill development such as sounding out various letter combinations, analyzing how to break words into prefixes and suffixes, and learning new vocabulary words. Only 15 minutes centered on the story they were reading. The lesson included virtually no imaginative or meaningful context for the children. From their point of view, it was learning skills for the sake of learning skills and it was disconnected from their lives.

In the past I have watched this teacher use many methods to make a lesson more engaging, but she is no longer allowed to do so because school administrators believe it will distract students from preparing for the required high-stakes, annual tests. After watching her and many other teachers, it is clear to me that such controlled, textbook-driven lessons have not only diminished their enthusiasm but also served to lessen children's engagement in the learning process.

At an established charter school on the other side of the city, teachers don't follow a lock-step curriculum. Every morning in a combined fourth- and fifth-grade classroom, children cluster around a model of the Los Angeles River they have been constructing for several months. The project began with a field trip to the river, where ecology experts showed the students how it is being rejuvenated. In the classroom model, water taken from the river travels from a raised tank filled with local plants down a twisting path into a glass tank inhabited by crayfish and more riverbed plants. The water is then pumped back up to the first tank. As the children monitor the crayfish, scrub the sides of the tank, and rearrange parts of the model, their teacher, preparing for the beginning of class, watches to make sure they interact with the crayfish appropriately and that they do not use soap to clean the tanks. She has a sixth sense about when to intervene. The purpose of the project is to study the river in all its forms, including the centuries of history that unfolded along its banks. As the class studies different periods of California history, the scenery along the river model changes. Two teachers share the class of 60 students and they have carefully tied the river project to state curriculum standards. But by taking the children to the river and bringing components of the ecosystem back to their classroom, instead of teaching solely from textbooks, they have brought biology, ecology, and history to life. They have engaged their students imaginatively and they also have connected those lessons in tangible ways to contemporary issues and their community.

On one visit to this classroom, I watched some of the children reading ecologically themed mysteries in preparation for writing their own. The beginning bell had yet to ring, but the students were there, eager to be part of the activities. Yes, they do worksheets on language usage, mathematical operations, and other standard requirements—they, too, must take the standardized tests so they need to be familiar with the exam format. But most of the time, these children are engaged and fascinated by what they are doing, and their test scores do not suffer because of their integrated, creative curriculum.

I have been asked again and again by Chinese parents and educators how to include creativity in their classrooms and in their children's lives. Yet when I ask them what they wish to accomplish, they usually say they want to replace exam-oriented learning rather than describing what they would like to see in its place. In the United States, definitions of creativity are all over the map, but people don't hesitate to try. Most can readily point to creative things their children or others have done and said—a story written about a multicolored caterpillar, an unusual way of describing something, a narrative written for an English class, an imagined dialogue between two historic figures, creating a small business, or developing a tutoring program for neighborhood children. In the world beyond family and the classroom, they readily point to iconic structures built by such visionaries as Frank Gehry, technical advances in electronics, or particular art and music that moves them. That does not occur in China.

I began to realize that I needed to understand exactly how Chinese educators and friends define "creativity." The Ministry of Education, the body that oversees all education in China, usually frames it in economic terms, primarily as the ability to create original inventions and research. As early as 1998, the ministry issued an action plan that began with these words:

> Currently, and in the near future, the lack of creative talent capable of international leadership has already become the greatest restriction in our nation's creative ability and competitiveness.[4]

The plan emphasized the international shift to a knowledge-based economy that would create "dramatic change...in humanity's economic and social life." It continued, "In the approaching 21st century, new advanced technologies at the core of the knowledge economy will occupy the most important position" and will depend on educational development and advanced knowledge creation.

The Chinese government has been well aware of the need to stimulate more innovative education and move away from memorization and questions that demand text-specific answers. A year after the initial 1998 recommendations, the education ministry began suggesting curriculum reform:

> There must be a reform in the training of human talent. We must enthusiastically begin the use of heuristic methods and discussion in order to stimulate students' independent thinking and their innovative and creative consciousness...We must make students become aware of, and understand, the process of knowledge production and development; we must cultivate students' scientific spirit and creative habits of thought; we must place emphasis on students ability to collect and manage

information, their ability to gather new knowledge and to analyze and solve problems.[5]

Serious efforts to reform classroom practice followed. Textbooks were modernized, and teacher retraining efforts, begun first in selected schools in each province, have been occurring gradually in other schools. However, the questions I continue to be asked suggest that parents and some teachers want to see more far-reaching change and that it will not come until there is a major overhaul of exam requirements. The 1999 curriculum reform eliminated junior high school entrance exams, but high school and college entrance exams remain.

Dongyan, with whom I have had many long conversations, worries that not enough is changing; by the time Chinese students are in high school, it is too late to learn to challenge what others tell them and develop truly independent thought habits. She says many parents still tell their children repeatedly, "Your job is to study the classroom material."

In 2011, I interviewed ten parents and educators I'd known for years, asking them a set of open-ended questions to unearth what they meant by the term "creativity." Pondering these questions with great seriousness, they often thought in silence for a noticeable length of time before responding, seemingly unsure how to describe something creative. Often they named a school activity that was slightly different from the norm, like the weather report Wang Yan's daughter gave that was not tied to her textbooks.

One mother, whose son attended a junior high school for foreign languages known to have a richer curriculum than most schools, said the students were required to present daily reports in different classes and state their own opinions. (This is definitely the exception, rather than standard policy, in my experience.) Another parent mentioned that her child helped select articles by other students for a school paper and edited them with the teacher's guidance. Several of these activities struck me as opportunities for learning responsibility and leadership rather than examples of creative expression. They provide students with the chance to do something new, to stretch, and in that sense these activities engage their enthusiasm. But are the students being challenged in their thinking?

The concept of creativity seems so foreign to their tradition-based culture that when I asked what they did at home to engage their children's imagination and inspire creativity, they also hesitated. They talked of things they did with their children, but did not really regard those as creative. Yet I thought many of the activities they described certainly could tap a child's imagination or evoke creative thinking.

One couple, for instance, encourage their upper-grade child to engage in a variety of activities and experiences and then discuss them. They watch documentaries on the Discovery and National Geographic channels (yes, they are available in China) and invite people from different walks of life to their home. They buy Legos, which the boy loves, and books about science. When I last visited, he was experimenting with how successful various types of soil were for growing plants, using the windowsill of his parents' bedroom. The father, Gao Qian, and his son take day trips to explore new areas by train or bus. Although his son loves these trips, Gao doesn't view this as engaging the boy's imagination.

My colleague Yang Jin, who teaches university English language courses, believes children must be active, independent learners. She wants her daughter to be able to search for information and apply the appropriate analysis. She and her husband often ask their daughter questions about her reading to encourage her to think more deeply and relate what she has read to other topics. When the girl read an autobiography of Mao Zedong, they asked her, "What do you think of his learning experience? Was it effective?" Yang Jin explained their motive: "Learning should lead to capability, versatility, and exploring things; not just memorizing information or being a recorder."[6]

Of all the parents and teachers I interviewed, Yang Jin seemed most confident about how to effectively engage her child. In first or second grade, for example, her daughter wrote and illustrated original stories that were put on a local newspaper blog for children. Yang Jin and her husband proposed that if she finished enough stories, they would arrange to compile them in a little book to give to children who did not have many books.

Probing a little deeper into Yang Jin's background, I discovered she was a parent with one of the most creative graduate school experiences I've heard of among Chinese educators. The chair of her English department invited a teaching group from a Hong Kong university for intensive English lessons during a seven-day camp. They were divided into teams, and she and a Hong Kong student had to create English-speaking activities and games each day. If their team members did not know important English vocabulary words, the pair had to devise ways to teach them. Yang Jin said it was a completely new experience for her. She and her partner "had to strain our minds to think up ideas and then convince the Hong Kong students that they could do them and that they were useful."

For Liu Jiantao, a friend with a son in junior high school, creativity is "the ability to think differently from others." In China, however, from the earliest grades, "If a child has an original idea, then the teacher says it is not realistic; that it is not possible to carry out," Liu Jiantao said. "Chinese kids [learn to see] their original idea as a problem, rather than as something creative or exciting."

I think it may be more complicated. Chinese educators who discuss social and cultural differences between China and the United States emphasize the importance of not standing out in a crowd in their country. One father, though outspoken about the deadening nature of schools, nonetheless believes it's important his son does not "stand out as different; it exerts too much pressure on kids to do that." Instead, he and his wife encourage intellectual curiosity at home and toeing the line at school.

Fan Hao, a young English language instructor from a prestigious university, pointed out that the Western tradition of individuals expressing an opinion has been historically dangerous in China. When she asks her undergraduates what they have been taught, they invariably say to "follow the crowd," "don't stand out," despite the pressure to excel. "This attitude makes people less tolerant of criticism," Fan Hao said. "If people inside the group criticize, then they are asked, 'Are you Chinese?' The implication is that if you are Chinese you wouldn't criticize other Chinese."[7] How can this be, though, if Chinese teachers critique each other freely? And if Americans pride themselves on taking individual stands, why do U.S. teachers avoid criticizing others or being critiqued by them?

In a study of 451 undergraduates from two major mainland China cities—Beijing and Guangzhou—Elisabeth Rudowicz and Xiao-Gong Yue found that mainland students identified the core characteristics of creativity in ways similar to a Westerner's perspective.[8] These were as follows: originality, innovativeness, thinking and observational skills, flexibility, willingness to try, self-confidence, and imagination. However, unlike most Westerners, they rated these traits low on a desirability scale. In other words, although the students had relatively parallel views about what comprises creativity, they did not value those qualities. Only one, "good thinking" was rated within the top seven qualities considered the most important for a Chinese person to possess.[9] "Imaginative" and "individualistic" were rated the lowest of all possible traits. The findings were similar for graduate students from Hong Kong and Taipei, additional cities included in the study because they have somewhat different educational systems from mainland China.

What, in fact, does creativity involve? Can it be taught? Some say no. Others say we all have it innately. Eric Maisel, a creativity coach, holds that everyone has the potential to be creative and imaginative. Whether or not that potential is manifested is another matter.[10] Many believe it can be taught or nurtured. "The real story of creativity is more difficult and strange than many overly optimistic accounts have claimed," writes Mihaly Csikszentmihalyi, a Hungarian psychology professor who has taught in the United States since the 1960s.

> For one thing . . . an idea or product that deserves the label 'creative' arises from the synergy of many sources and not only from the mind of a single person. It is easier to enhance creativity by changing conditions in the environment than by trying to make people think more creatively. And a genuinely creative accomplishment is almost never the result of a sudden insight, a light bulb flashing on in the dark, but comes after years of hard work.[11]

Jane Healy, author of *Your Child's Growing Mind*,[12] cites a number of characteristics of creativity. The most salient qualities in an educational setting, she argues, are the ability to be intensely absorbed in activities, the ability to combine things or ideas in new ways, and the ability to make independent decisions and follow through on them. At the Otis College of Art and Design in Los Angeles, teachers have identified several necessary components—risk, energy, the inner locus of control (outer locus is just sopping up others' ideas), and originality drawn from within and personally enacted.[13]

Csikszentmihalyi adds a critical ingredient—that for most people, ideas are often sparked during interaction with others, and that creative people are "especially good at ordering their lives so that what they do, when, and with whom will enable them to do their best work."[14] This, of course, requires the courage to take control of one's life and, within a school setting, to give students choices that enhance collaboration as well as independent thinking and work. Being able to reach beyond obvious or predictable solutions, and acting to bring unusual concepts to fruition, either individually or collaboratively, are important now and will be critical as the twenty-first-century digital world unfolds.

Although many educators, psychologists, and others interested in fostering young children's potential believe one of the most important times to develop creativity is in the early years,[15,16] Yale University researchers Weihua Niu and Robert Sternberg believe creativity can be strengthened in an individual at any age. Their many investigations to determine whether tailored instruction can improve the artistic output of Chinese students have produced significant results.[17] Niu and Sternberg gave students in a vocational Beijing high school different sets of directions for a creative activity. Based on their previous research and that of others on the nature of Chinese culture,[18] especially the importance of collectivism and the fear of standing out, they hypothesized that telling everyone in a group that they should try to be creative would overcome any hesitancy about doing something different from the norm.

They worked with 96 students from the school. About 40 percent were enrolled in art-related programs such as hair-styling, tailoring, and sculpting; the others were in majors such as English and computer technology. Divided into three random groups, all were given identical packets of colorful stickers of three different shapes. But the instructions for each group differed in degrees of specificity. One group was merely told to make a design using the packets. Another also was given this added sentence: "Please try to be creative." The third group received both instructions plus this direction: "To be creative, you could fold or tear the stickers when necessary so that the shapes and sizes of the materials would not limit your creative expression." The resulting designs yielded remarkable results. The groups told to "try to be creative" and with more detailed instructions made more imaginative artwork than those who had simply been told to make a design. The students' course of study made no difference.[19] These findings suggest that merely creating a conducive environment, at least for older students, could help Chinese teachers lower the risk of standing out enough to generate originality among their students.

Adding these changes to what the Chinese government has already proposed in education could promote growth in creativity if the exam system were modified significantly. This has actually begun to happen. Beginning in 2008, the ministry permitted a small number of universities to admit 5 percent of their freshmen class using criteria other than exam scores, or in addition to them, on an experimental basis. Some of the foreign language school students in Nanjing, for instance, are not required to take exams. Meanwhile a massive government effort has been made to reform teachers' pedagogy, though change over the last decade has been incremental.

In the small village of An Shang on the edge of the Loess Plateau in north-central China, far from the cultural hub of Beijing, I observed teachers experiment with using materials the children would recognize, such as vegetables and pictures of refrigerators, washing machines, among other items to help connect math and language arts lessons to the children's everyday experiences. They told me it was so different from previous traditional lecture-dominated teaching that they had a difficult time understanding what to do.

The An Shang teachers described attending training sessions in small groups in the county seat to hear lectures about new theory and practice. There were no demonstrations, and they left the talks with almost no understanding of how to change their teaching practices. It took observing model lessons later in a nearby city to grasp the concepts. These teachers were serious about changing their methods, and although they still are constrained to teach to the test, what they were offering their rural students was more relevant than the lessons I had witnessed in earlier years at their school. Notably, though, these teachers had very small classes of 12–15 students because the population in rural villages is decreasing as parents migrate to large cities for jobs and because of the dropping birthrate.

In eastern China, teachers at a consolidated school that draws children from many villages in Anhui Province discussed the confusion they felt about the reforms. They, too, had attended lectures about engaging students in group work, and expressed considerable frustration because they had no idea how to do so or what it would accomplish. They said that with 50–60 students packed into a classroom, dividing them into smaller groups was proving to be a waste of time since they could not get around to all the groups. I realized that the teachers needed instruction on distinguishing when it is possible for students in large classes to participate productively in group work and what kinds of activities would clearly benefit from small groups. Furthermore, they needed to help children understand how to work in such a setting. These teachers needed much more professional development in order to change their practices in meaningful ways.

But by 2011, with a few exceptions such as An Shang, most classrooms I visited were virtually unchanged beyond surface adjustments such as a little student praise or group work so highly structured that children were still connected tightly to the text.

In urban areas, the most significant change has taken place in what are called "small-class" schools. Unlike the elite "key" schools that are oversubscribed with 40–50 students in one room, small-class schools, which are experimental, have no more than 24 students per room. In one such classroom I recently observed a math lesson taught without a textbook and with students working in groups. The teacher was practicing a demonstration lesson she would later present to teachers in a large school district in her city. The group structure, in contrast to traditional lessons, involved students in continuous, though limited and meticulously guided experimentation to help them comprehend a geometric concept. However, the teacher's final goal was to have them define the concept exactly as stated in their textbook. There was more student involvement than I'd seen in earlier years, and therefore a little imaginative engagement, but the activities were still highly scripted by the teacher, increment by increment to arrive at the prescribed correct answer. Almost no independent thinking took place.

Interestingly, although in practice these new teaching methods often differ only on the surface from previous lessons, there is already a backlash. A number of parents at those schools complain that such teaching is not tied closely enough to the high school and college entrance exams for their children to attain scores needed to qualify for a preferred college. Even a parent I know who is critical of the Chinese education system and is working hard to find an affordable college outside China for her high school-age son said the new method of teaching "isn't serious enough and has too many activities."

If taking risks and showing independence are characteristics of creativity, these qualities are emphasized at an early age in the United States. Toddlers are allowed to walk unsteadily and unaided, whereas in China parents and grandparents guide toddlers at every step so they won't trip or lose their balance and fall. Huang Ren Song, a colleague who is a nationally known early childhood education specialist, has observed during her many trips to the United States that young American children are allowed much more leeway and become much braver than Chinese preschoolers. Most American children are allowed to color and paint freely, admonished only to stay on the paper. Children's "why" questions and challenges are usually encouraged (although parents at some point may resort to saying, "Because I told you to"). At school, asking why they need to line up or do their work may not be allowed, but questioning why something works or why and how characters in a story could have acted differently are encouraged by most U.S. teachers.

Life in Chinese schools and homes is vastly different for multiple reasons. Though China is undergoing rapid change and economic development, many traditions remain a rich foundation for everyday Chinese life and education. As classroom techniques adapt to the demands of the twenty-first century, the United States and China can learn from each other and borrow some ideas, but education reforms cannot ignore the traditions and culture of each country.

12

Ready for the Future?

Students must learn how to learn, beginning in kindergarten. The top ten in-demand jobs for 2010 did not exist in 2004, according to Linda Darling-Hammond, professor of education at Stanford University and nationally known advocate for improving school quality. She also points out, "The new mission of schools is to prepare students to work at jobs that do not yet exist, creating ideas and solutions for products and problems that have not yet been identified, using technologies that have not yet been invented."[1] What is needed is a system that teaches deep subject-area knowledge while also valuing originality and flexibility of thinking. This is a daunting task for the education systems of China and the United States.

Middle-class American teenagers arrive at college armed with an ever-expanding toolkit—laptop computer, smart phone, gaming station, digital camera, and notepad, not to mention palm-sized players that hold a vast library of music and videos. They've been raised on instantaneous Internet access, and this is true not only in the United States and Europe, but also in China and the rest of the world. The result, says conceptual artist, curator, and teacher Ernesto Pujol, is nothing less than "a pivotal historical perceptual change" that requires a radical rethinking of teaching. In the persuasive opening essay of *Art School (Propositions for the 21st Century)*, Pujol argues that his art and design students must be taught in ways that match the interconnected, fast-changing, digital world in which they live, learn, and work.[2] I would argue that educators of all stripes, from elementary grades through graduate schools, must confront this challenge.

Ready or not, we have been catapulted into the Information Age. Knowledge and opinion are accessible to anyone with Internet access. The quantitative and qualitative change in how humans interact leaves older generations in wonder and disbelief. Young people, including those in poor communities and countries, know nothing else. Suddenly the richest and poorest among us can bypass social, cultural, and national boundaries. Economic interests are intertwined across the globe and the fortunes of whole countries swing rapidly as international competition shifts. Personal, social, and ethical values are continuously exposed to challenges from other belief systems while, at the same time, being enriched by the diversity of other people's experiences. How well we educate our children will determine their ability not only to compete in the twenty-first-century marketplace but also to enable them to help our societies thrive and improve.

Today's students are restless about ideas, objects, practices, and pedagogies, says Steven Henry Maddoff, senior critic at Yale University's School of Art. They arrive wanting "more porosity, irritated by bureaucratic weight, impatient for new shapes."[3] The most engaging schooling, today as in the past, involves complex, real-world learning. Before, it was only the exceptional teacher or school who offered this. Now this type of teaching is critical for all students if they are to succeed. "It is an emphasis on what students can do with knowledge, rather than what units of knowledge they have, that best describes the essence of 21st century skills," says Elena Silva, senior policy analyst at Education Sector, a nonpartisan think tank that examines education policy and reforms, and explores new possibilities.[4] Studies by research organizations such as the Organisation for Economic Co-operation and Development (OECD) show that complex thinking and analytical skills are entwined in learning at every stage of development.[5] Students need to learn basic skills within rich, experiential contexts. They can learn to develop well-structured paragraphs while writing a letter to the school board. Lessons like the Los Angeles River project in the Los Angeles fourth/fifth-grade classroom, described in Chapter 11, weave in new skills and basic knowledge while teaching children how to investigate complex concepts. Bringing subjects alive helps children learn in lasting ways.

If we don't know what jobs to prepare our children for, we do know that certain skills will be critical. Toni Wagner, a former teacher whose Ph.D. dissertation at Harvard focused on the current needs and work requirements of U.S. corporations, found that the demands are the same across the board—from high-end corporate offices to assembly lines.[6] Company organizational structure has been flattened. Work is organized in networks of cross-functional teams that collaborate on specific projects. It is defined by the task or problem the team needs to solve or the goal it wants to accomplish. Solutions are not prescribed. The team must develop them. Moreover, tomorrow's task may require addressing an entirely different problem set, with a different set of team members.

Corporation and business leaders of all kinds invariably told Wagner that they most value curiosity and inquisitiveness in their employees. "Creativity and innovation are key factors not only in solving problems but also in developing new or improved products and services," he explains, adding that graduating students need to be able to "think in disciplined ways, but also . . . have a burning curiosity, a lively imagination, and can engage others empathetically."[7] They need to do this not just within their own organization but across national boundaries and languages as well.

Many U.S. and multinational employers already require workers to be able to design, evaluate, and manage their own projects, frame and solve problems using multiple resources, collaborate strategically with others, communicate in many forms, and find and analyze information to help develop new products and ideas.

Students who are not adequately prepared for these realities will be unable to compete globally. Yet for the most part, the United States and China are weighted down by outdated education systems. Yes, there *are* bright spots and many teachers who are trying to meet the challenge. But much more is needed. Both countries must work urgently to update their schools, and learning from each other's strengths as well as flaws could speed the transformation. U.S. policy makers, for instance, could learn from the Chinese the debilitating effect of relying on narrow, standardized tests for educational advancement. The establishments of both countries should take note of the surging adulation of Steve Jobs as a creative icon among young people in China.[8]

To enable students to think critically about real challenges and to support their ideas with solid information and reasoning, schools in both countries must move away from textbook-driven, teacher-centered instructional methods. "Beginning in primary school, students need to have more chances to DO things, not just sit and listen," said Wang Yan, an English instructor in Nanjing who has a young child. "They need to experiment and get involved. They need to use their hands and bodies and minds. They need to go into the neighborhood and the city to observe."[9]

Science instruction from the earliest grades needs to guide students to conduct actual experiments and inquiries, to record procedures and observations, to ask questions, to analyze real data, and to propose evidence-based interpretations. In the social sciences, children need to learn how to weave together factual information and theory, to analyze the complexities of national and community issues, and to discuss solutions. Also critically important are strong literacy skills for learning important information and concepts, and for communicating ideas and solutions persuasively. In both countries, any measurement of competency must assess a student's ability to engage in complex learning and to apply theories to real problems.

In general, Chinese students have a greater depth of basic knowledge than do American students. They study science—biology, physics, and chemistry—throughout junior and senior high school. Math is learned in more complexity beginning in the primary grades, and reading comprehension involves probing an author's meanings more deeply than is considered important in most U.S. classrooms. Such strengths in the Chinese curriculum can be studied to explore how they might be adapted to enhance the American learning environments. It is also true that Chinese students, from preschool on, are expected to focus and work hard, and they are able to apply themselves to schoolwork inside and outside class much more readily than their U.S. counterparts. This attentiveness and discipline arise from Chinese culture itself and from ancient educational traditions that would be impossible to imitate. Experienced U.S. teachers know, however, that classroom behavior and student self-confidence and learning improve markedly when students are engaged in serious and active learning. Many such teachers know how to provide active learning, but are often hampered because they are required to use "teacher proof" lessons that obliterate their ability to draw from their extensive knowledge.

Chinese teachers, on the other hand, could benefit from investigating U.S. strategies and emulating some of them. Unlike the Chinese, most American students benefit from working in groups, where students often achieve greater mastery of their subject than if they had learned the lesson in lecture-centered classrooms. By collaborating, they learn to appreciate diverse skills, to ask questions, and to express their opinions. U.S. teachers bring in speakers and materials from the world beyond school and organize educational trips to such places as nature preserves and museums to augment classroom lessons. Students have the advantage of developing projects and class presentations using a variety of formats and multiple resources from inside and outside the school, and teachers encourage students to express their opinions and to connect class learning to their lives. Some Chinese and American teachers have made short trips to each other's countries and classrooms over the years, but most of these exchanges have tended to yield quick-fix ideas that are seldom sustainable in a different culture. Video conferencing halfway around the world and using other digital media offer a possibility for substantive and longer-term interactions between Chinese and American educators that could yield positive results.

Since the devastating Cultural Revolution ended in 1976—when schools were closed for ten years—the Chinese government has put considerable effort into improving both teacher education and students' educational opportunities. The government has raised the status, qualifications, and salaries of teachers; increased the number of colleges; and attempted to move away from lecture-based pedagogy. Central to these improvements is the hour or more each day set aside, in every school, for collaboration among teachers, who observe and critique each other to improve their lessons. In the United States, support for professional growth is more limited. Elementary teachers have, at best, an hour or two a week to gather with some of their colleagues, but this is usually for such required duties as reviewing test data and curriculum standards. U.S. high school teachers are given three to five hours a week of preparation time, but most often use it for correcting papers or getting materials for the next class. Teacher collaboration is not a regular part of U.S. education culture. Some professional development communities have formed, often as a result of school–university partnerships, but these are generally short-lived because they are supported by external grants.

What then can be done to move our schools forward, to better prepare young people for the challenges they face in the Information Age? Many solutions will, of course, evolve over time as schools transition to new realities, but there are plenty of previously tried solutions that can be applied now in the United States and China.

It is also essential that both nations more effectively address the inequality of scholastic opportunities. A learning revolution cannot take place just by changing the education of the elites; everyone needs to participate if both nations are to prosper in the decades ahead. It is impossible to address in detail such large, social needs here, but several areas can be targeted for instructional reforms aimed at giving all of the children the ability to compete in the twenty-first century, and also to work in collaboration with people around the globe. The sections that follow offer several substantive suggestions, including integrating digital media into all learning, shifting classroom instruction to active learning and team projects, and developing assessments that measure complex learning. Teachers and principals, who will implement all these changes, must be supported with strong preparatory courses and ongoing, substantive professional development throughout their careers. If this sounds expensive, the social and economic price of not moving forward is far more costly.

Media Literacy

Jeff Share, one of the many educators and teachers I have interviewed, emphasized it's critical to help children understand digital tools and the power of the World Wide Web. Share, an advisor for the teacher preparation program at the University of California at Los Angeles, works with beginning teachers in urban schools. His eclectic background—ten years as a photojournalist in Latin America, collaboration with a Catholic nun on media literacy in schools, and many attempts to help schools use computers in substantive ways—informs his efforts to help new teachers succeed in modern classrooms, where, he contends, "computers are being used like expensive crayons in most schools."[10]

Even more important than putting computers to better use, Share says, is teaching students of all ages "critical media literacy," to learn to evaluate the torrents of information being poured onto the Internet.[11,12] They need to be aware that anyone—with or without credentials or knowledge—can send messages or post information that may be inaccurate, if not downright wrong or malicious. They need to learn how to judge what they are seeing and hearing, to sift through it and find the important, reliable material.

It is also imperative that people of all ages learn how to communicate in the instantaneous digital universe, to think carefully about what they are saying and to whom they are speaking before posting a message. Share cites the cautionary example of a UCLA undergraduate who posted a video on YouTube criticizing and mocking Asian students. An avalanche of negative feedback calling her message racist, and even death threats, led her to apologize and take it down, but it was too late. She left the university. "Probably 20 million people saw her video," says Share. In a predigital world, she might have made a verbal comment to a friend or two. Now, an off-the-cuff or ill-considered post on the Internet can go viral—with unforeseen consequences.

The message: Teachers and what they teach must adapt to today's fast-paced world in thoughtful ways. "Being able to just read and write is a joke now," Share points out. "Of course, you need those. But you need so much more to be functionally literate. Education needs . . . to embrace digital media technologies, use them, and at the same time, help kids think critically about them. Critical thought must be part of the game."

Embracing Technology

Despite these challenges, the potential of digital media is, of course, enormous. Students, beginning in first grade or even kindergarten, need to learn to use computers as powerful, creative tools—not just for entertainment. Gradually they must learn how computers can help them generate ideas, hunt for information and analyze its accuracy and validity, put together substantive reports, link theories they are learning to real-world situations, and present their ideas to wider audiences. Share suggests harnessing the cell phones that are now stuffed in students' pockets and backpacks because they are banned in classrooms in both countries. Most of these phones have digital cameras that could be used in comprehensive ways to advance data collection and communicate ideas. Even more is possible with newer generations of Internet-accessible smart phones.

In a large number of U.S. schools, basic computers are used for skill development. Schools in wealthier American communities often have more advanced digital equipment but not necessarily a considered strategy for using it. A classroom full of iPads is a colossal waste without a plan that uses them to augment the curriculum. In China, urban elementary schools tend to have a computer in each classroom that teachers use to display work sheets and textbook pages, and junior and senior high school students are taught computer applications. Some rural schools have Internet access for teachers to retrieve lesson materials, but if we are going to help all students use electronic media wisely, students need access to the Internet within the context of a comprehensive curriculum, absent in both countries.

Interactive Learning

What Chinese and American students learn in elementary and high school also must change. That does not mean throwing out everything, but it does mean reevaluating what students need to master during 12 or more years of education. The knowledge economy—that the Chinese government began to see as important as early as 1998, and has been a central topic of discussion at many U.S. education conferences for just as long—demands radical change.

Forward-thinking education experts in both countries say students learn best when they develop and use a sound knowledge base in interactive learning situations. Parroting back what the text or the teacher says is ineffective. Students need to be able to assess real issues and support their solutions with solid information and reasoning. This, of course, means rigorously learning how to read, write, calculate numbers, and analyze, but students must also be taught to apply these skills in practical ways in the earliest grades—every day.

Beginning teacher Mohammed Choudhury successfully combined this method with critical media literacy in an impoverished, heavily Hispanic Los Angeles junior high school. It is well documented that children who aren't proficient in English by the time they reach sixth grade usually do not fare well. They are disheartened by their educational prospects and have negative feelings about their abilities. But Choudhury's sixth-graders had new worlds open to them as he challenged the class of English-language learners to explore their social environment in new and critical ways.

Choudhury assigned his students the job of investigating what was reported in newspapers, on TV, and in promotional materials about their section of the city. They discovered the reported information was invariably negative, highlighting the words "poor," "gang-ridden," "overcrowded," "drugs," and "criminals" and displaying pictures that reinforced those messages. Despite the neighborhood's tarnished reputation in the media, they discovered that it had some wonderful schools, plenty of trees and well-kept apartments, Cuban restaurants, and more. The assignment taught them to recognize that messages are always written from someone's point of view, which may be limited if not inaccurate.

Choudhury went further, empowering these students to challenge the negative image, to let the world know there was more to their neighborhood than gangs. They took walking field trips to document, block by block, the resources of the community. They interviewed and photographed community members. Back in class, they discussed and analyzed their material again and again, interrogating their findings. They created a PowerPoint presentation (an application that usually lays dormant in most classroom computers) describing their neighborhood's strengths, which they shared with other classes at their school and then at an education conference at UCLA on the other side of the city. In the process, Choudhury's students not only greatly increased their academic skills and self-respect, a majority of them also improved their ability to speak and write in English enough to be moved into mainstream courses, putting them on a path for academic success.[13,14]

Global Awareness

The knowledge economy also requires students to be culturally attuned to multiple languages, diverse perspectives, and a variety of values. In all elementary schools across China, students begin studying English in third grade, and many schools are starting these lessons even earlier. Chinese children continue studying English through high school. U.S. schools are slowly incorporating language study in earlier grades, primarily though voluntary bilingual programs, but unfortunately the many children who speak a language other than English at home are often asked to check their native tongue at the school door rather than bring its richness to the learning environment. In some parts of the United States with highly diverse populations, children and their parents are gradually learning to interact with and appreciate people of different cultures. The Chinese do not yet have this advantage, since 90 percent of the population is Han Chinese and minority groups are generally marginalized. Chinese children from more affluent families, however, often have contact with cultures beyond their borders through home stays and exchange programs. These initiatives are all rather limited considering the speed of globalization.

Two programs among many that can offer schools a global perspective are the International Baccalaureate schools and De Orilla a Orilla. The International Baccalaureate (IB) Programme, originally begun in Geneva, Switzerland, in 1968 for the children of United Nations delegates and employees as well as international workers from many countries, stresses a curriculum of topical units and themes that address worldwide interests and challenges. Now available in schools in 141 countries, including China and the United States, IB teachers are required to use an inquiry-and-analysis approach to curriculum material and students must study in depth a language other than their native tongue.[15] Louis Carrillo, principal of Meyler Elementary School in the Los Angeles school district that is a candidate for the IB program, said he and his teachers are in its multiyear planning process to determine whether they can adapt their curriculum. They have long had a successful Spanish–English immersion program for students who want to become fully bilingual and biliterate, and they now want to offer students a globally focused curriculum and learning skills that will empower them to thrive in the Information Age. One of their challenges is to transform their traditional pedagogical teaching methods to inquiry-driven teaching. They understand it is an arduous path, but have committed to the task.

A cutting-edge project begun in 1985, De Orilla a Orilla (Spanish for "From Shore to Shore") provides an educational networking platform for collaboration between teachers and schools in various countries. It facilitates connections for planning and sharing data and observations among participants through email and computer-based conferencing. In one project, elementary through high school students in the United States, Puerto Rico, Argentina, South Africa, China, and Australia explored and analyzed what it's like to move to a new place. The goal was to use research to develop suggestions on how to make schools better for newcomers. Participants asked older people in their communities about their experiences of moving to a new town or school when they were young. What had they hoped the new place would be like, what was it really like, and who helped them adapt to the change? They then asked the same questions of a schoolmate who had moved, and then combined their research with classes in their school and in other countries. Finally, they decided on ways to make their school better for newcomers. Another Orillas project, connecting math to students' everyday lives and their communities, has evolved over several years and includes 27 high schools and elementary schools in 14 countries, from Ecuador to Bangladesh to Egypt. The potential for this type of international collaboration is great and provides students with important challenges. When they write to others from a distinct geographic, cultural, or linguistic reality, Orillas staff point out, they can't assume that the other students share the same assumptions and background information, so they need to learn how to step back and rethink the world in which they live.[16]

Inquiry and Analysis

If we are to educate our young to become innovators able to meet the challenges ahead, they not only need to master basic skills but also need to learn the art of inquiry and the discipline of analysis. Although I see much more open-ended instruction focused on inquiry and analysis in U.S. schools than in China, one recent lesson given to Chinese second-graders shows it is possible to use this method even in the earliest grades in both countries. But it requires a teacher who is thoroughly versed in the subject matter.

I observed Liang Na, a math teacher in one of the small-class schools in eastern China, skillfully lead her students through trial-and-error problem solving and group interactions that helped them master the subject while being imaginatively engaged.

The lesson began when Teacher Liang entered the room briskly and exchanged greetings with 22 second-graders.

"I have a question for you," she told them. "If I want to find Grade Five, where do you suggest I should go?" Her topic for the day was arrays, an arrangement of objects in rows and columns, though she never introduced that word. She wanted them to comprehend the concept in the physical setting of their school and classroom as well as with two-dimensional examples projected on the video screen and in their textbooks.

A few hands went up.

"Lin Miao."

"Uhh, I suggest you should look for it on the fourth floor up there," Lin Miao said, hesitantly pointing toward the floor above their classroom.

"Oh, the fourth floor there, right? Very good. What if I want to find the classroom of Grade Six?"

Several hands shot up and one student blurted out, "Teacher, let me answer." The students were already engaged, thinking about the world they know well.

"Ok, you tell us."

"Go upstairs this way or that way."

"Which floor?"

"The third floor."

Liang continued to ask about places within the school building and pointed out that they are called "locations" in real life. She then set a puzzle for them: One of the students in the class said hello to her at the school gate when she was arriving. She wanted them to guess who it was.

"I'll give you some clues. He sits in the third row, the second desk. Who might he be? He is the second one in the third row." The students, eager to be part of the game, jumped in, already more eager to participate and take more of a risk being wrong than any group of students I have seen in China.

"He might be Zheng Zihan," one child said.

"Zheng Zihan, stand up please. You count the rows for us, okay?" He counted the rows of desks, first row, second row, third row. Next Liang asked him to count the desks, the first then the second—where he was sitting.

"Any other guesses?" she asked. Hands went up and students identified others they think are in the second seat of the third row. The clue she has purposely omitted is which row to count first. Is the first row on the left side of the room, the right side, or in the front? It is an important piece of information, and she wanted them to discover it themselves so they gain experience solving a problem by accumulating evidence. The children began to frown as they named several more students who they think are sitting in the second seat of a row. There can't be that many students in the same seat.

One student finally mentioned "the front," and the teacher responded, "What do you mean by 'the front'?" Liang asked the girl to count the rows, and she did, ever so hesitantly. The girl counted the rows from the front of the room and the seats from left to right.

"Do you think she is right counting this way?"

"Wrong," they said. The criticism had a friendly tone. Although the student was a bit embarrassed, she was not ashamed; the puzzle was like a good-natured game. She began again, but the teacher stopped her. The confusion had gone on long enough even though they were enjoying it.

"You can't count rows in one direction and desks in the row in an opposite order. I have called three students to answer this question. None of them knows why a particular student is in the second desk in the third row."

Unlike children in most Chinese classrooms, Liang's students have been taking risks, giving answers they know may be wrong. Her students clearly trust her. She challenged them further.

"Now, I want you to think it over: Why can we find so many people when it seems only one person meets the criteria? What is the reason? Get yourselves into your groups of four and discuss this with each other. Group leaders should take charge. Think it over: Why does such a thing happen?"

Liang moved from one group to the next, providing clues and especially asking where they are starting to count from. "Start from this corner." "Where do you think the front is?" She skillfully led them to solve the puzzle with more revealing questions.

After letting them discuss the problem and disagree a little with each other, she called them back together.

"Okay, can anybody tell us your discussion results? Why are there so many different cases? You try," she said, calling on a girl in a pink sweater.

"Because they counted in different directions," the student replied, quite sure of herself. When the teacher asked her to be more specific, the girl pointed out that everyone has been counting in different directions, some from right to left, some from left to right, some from the front near the blackboard and video screen, others from the bulletin board at the back of the room.

Teacher Liang restated the girl's answer and moved to the textbook supplements displayed on the video screen. She projected a textbook page of cartoon-like animals doing exercises in rows. The starting point was given. She had the students select an animal and tell their group its location. She then had them locate specific animals as a whole class, with one student at a time identifying them. She helped the hesitant few. Next the students tried a diagram for locating apartments in large buildings and then books on shelves. The last textbook activity was a numbered grid into which they must place different geometric shapes. "Put a pink triangle in the third box of the fourth row." "Put a blue square in the first box of the second row." By the end, all the students seemed to understand how to locate items on the screen and in their textbook.

However, Teacher Liang was not through. The final activity assessed whether they now could apply this learning to themselves. She had the group leaders give each student a slip of paper on which she had written a new seat assignment, phrased in terms of the classroom as an array. One needed to move to the third seat in the second row, another needed to move to the fourth seat in the first row, and so on, with the starting point clearly given. They milled around the classroom hunting for their new seats. Some found them immediately after counting; some wandered a bit, consulted with others, and found their place. But several could not find their seats, which gave Liang an instant assessment of who thoroughly grasped these concepts and who did not.

Subject Matter Knowledge

Teacher Liang managed to create a lesson that allowed second-grade students to see a problem spatially, work together to try to find solutions, test their ideas, and extrapolate with textbook diagrams. Finally, she had them try to solve a similar problem in a game like musical chairs. She provided a structured, yet semi-open-ended situation to introduce, develop, and cement the mathematical concept, and in a way that encouraged these young children to think. Liang was guiding them along a path to becoming independent thinkers, able to use evidence to work out solutions.

This kind of teaching requires mastery of the subject matter. Liang Na was able to lead her students through this inquiry, in part, because she understood arrays. She understood where their thinking was going wrong, and could help them discover what they needed to examine. Lecturing and telling students the answers is easy; leading them through complex thinking requires much more subject matter knowledge.

In China, all teachers—in elementary, junior, and senior high school—specialize in a subject. In the United States, only junior and senior high school teachers specialize; elementary teachers do not. In studying for a teaching credential they learn a smattering of how to teach reading and language arts, math, science, social science, art, music, health, and physical education. Most American elementary school teachers are missing the subject-specific knowledge necessary to lead students to investigate and analyze topics in depth. This raises a serious question: Should they specialize in a subject like their Chinese peers do, or is it better for them to specialize in knowing their students very well? These are trade-offs that should not be treated lightly.

No matter how this problem is resolved, all teachers in the United States would benefit from the collaborative teacher groups, like those in China, to help them analyze what topics and skills need teaching in more depth and devising means to enhance their own teaching.

Measuring Learning

How can we measure the complex skills learned in Liang's classroom in China and Choudhury's in the United States? Assessments are an essential part of any school program. They help us understand how well, and what, students are learning and where teachers need to adjust curriculum to help address concepts students don't understand fully. However, most exams today measure only whether students have learned particular bits of knowledge. That is certainly not sufficient for today or the future. Educational assessments drive instruction and making them congruent with our goals is a critical need. A number of innovative, often subject-specific assessment instruments have been developed, and the virtual worlds and hypothetical situations that can be created by computer programs can be easily adapted for assessment purposes.[17] Many are already in the development stage; others are deemed too expensive or too complex by policy makers and education administrators. However, cost needs to be assessed by looking at total expenditures per student and the value that more complex and accurate assessments would provide in the long run.

The International Baccalaureate Programme has required performance assessments and individual student portfolios for more than 30 years.[18] These and other methods of complex evaluation are well regarded by those who have used them. They require students to demonstrate their grasp of subjects in various formats: written, orally, and with experimental data. They are scored by teachers who have been trained to assess the learning. When used on a large scale, such as for the IB high school diploma program or the California teacher credentialing process, examiners are trained and paid for their services.

Expense often determines testing methods. The U.S. Government Accounting Office estimated that in 2003, North Carolina's multiple-choice, machine-scored assessments cost 60 cents each, and Massachusetts spent seven dollars apiece for tests with some open-ended questions. The College Work and Readiness Assessment (CWRA), a 90-minute open-ended test that is scored by individuals and yields much more realistic data about student skills, costs 40 dollars a test.[19] Though 40 dollars is considered too costly by education policy makers, it is 0.44 percent—less than one-half of one percent—of the approximately $9,000 per pupil spent annually in the United States.[20] Governmental agencies in both the United States and China need to open their thinking to assessments that will enhance student learning and teaching processes, not limit them.

Professional Development

Fundamental to all of these suggestions is substantive professional development. "Teachers are often asked to do things without being given the necessary tools," says Jennifer Yuré, former principal and science coordinator for the Pasadena, California, school district. A half day in-service is nearly useless. Teachers need substantive, ongoing professional development. To become an IB school, for instance, teachers and administrators must participate in several years of preparation, with input from IB experts and collaboration among themselves to adapt curriculum. They must learn to teach inquiry lessons, which requires teachers to experience carrying out their own inquiries and then learning to develop inquiry-focused lessons. Just as students need guided experiential learning, teachers need to be respected for the knowledge they have and also mentored in new ways of teaching. This requires time, something the Chinese teacher collaborative groups provide.

Countries that have steeply improved their students' achievement in recent years invest heavily in teachers' professional development, points out Linda Darling-Hammond in her book about education in the digital world. In those nations "teachers have time for collaboration, collective planning, lesson study, peer coaching, developing curriculum and assessments, and joint examination of student work."[21] Countries such as Belgium, Hungary, and Finland, she says, provide time for professional development in the teachers' workday or week and opportunities for them to analyze and improve their teaching practice. In Singapore teachers have "time and support to study and evaluate their own teaching strategies and school programs" and to share findings with their colleagues.[22] In contrast, in the United States, no such system supports this type of teacher development.

Where We Need to Head

Throughout my travels in the United States and China, I've seen that the best learning happens when basic skills and complex thinking are taught in combination and when the material is relevant to the students' lives. Young children develop sound writing techniques best when they write about things important to them. Students grasp math concepts best when they connect the basics with complex problem solving. Pockets of such teaching exist in both countries, but both the Chinese and American education systems need to assure that complex thinking and skill learning are entwined at every stage of schooling.

Change comes slowly. Nevertheless, since the 1990s I've watched Chinese classrooms become livelier places, with textbooks of more interest to students and teachers involving students more actively in lessons. U.S. schools have begun to provide time for teachers to work together and to realize the importance of teacher collaboration. In some U.S. charter schools, free from the many constraints imposed on the rest of the schools, interactive learning has created enthusiastic, serious learners. Both systems, however, are weighted down by exams—China with a culture of exams it is trying to move away from, and the United States refusing to look seriously beyond simplistic testing. But China and the United States each have myriad strengths within their schools.

Imagine what could happen if Chinese and U.S. educators and school administrators drew from the most successful methods of each system, learning from each other to develop curricula and pedagogy that engage students' imaginations and that teach them to tap their creative and problem-solving abilities, infusing academic work with thoughtful, original thinking. Collaborating cross-culturally, in the process, would benefit everyone.

Children in the United States and China have enormous potential. They also have a connection to a digital universe that adults don't fully comprehend. I would love to see both countries connect that potential and the developing, international digital world into planned comprehensive schooling that addresses twenty-first-century realities. Schooling where students are engaged and teachers and administrators are part of learning communities focused on improving their own teaching.

These are demanding and stimulating challenges. If we are willing to meet them, our young people and future generations will be the beneficiaries.

Notes

Chapter 1

1. Ingersoll, Richard M. *A Comparative Study of Teacher Preparation and Qualifications in Six Nations.* CPRE Policy Briefs. RB-47. Philadelphia: Consortium for Policy Research in Education, 2007.
2. Li, Jun. "Chinese Teachers' Constructions of Their Roles in Developing Curriculum." Paper presented at the 11th International Congress on Mathematical Education (ICME-11), Monterrey, Mexico, 2008. Retrieved from http://dg.icme11.org/tsg/show/18#inner-4 on July 10, 2011.
3. Ingersoll. "Comparative Study."
4. Wang, Xiao-lei, Ronan Bernas, and Philippe Eberhard. "Maternal Teaching Strategies in Four Cultural Communities: Implications for Early Childhood Teachers." *Journal of Early Childhood Research* 3.3 (2005):269–288. Print.
5. Wang et al. "Maternal Teaching Strategies," 285.
6. Stevenson, Harold. "Learning from Asian Schools." *Scientific American* December 1992, 72.
7. Confucius. *The Chinese Classics: Translated into English with Preliminary Essays and Explanatory Notes by James Legge. Vol. 1. The Life and Teachings of Confucius.* London: Trubner, 1896. Retrieved from http://oll.libertyfund.org/title/2270/213620 on March 04, 2011.
8. Li, Tianchen, translator. *A Collection of Confucius' Sayings: An English-Chinese Bilingual Textbook.* Jinan, China: Qi Lu Press, 1988, 123.
9. Li, Jin, and Qi Wang. "Perceptions of Achievement and Achieving Peers in U.S. and Chinese Kindergartners." *Social Development* 13.3 (2004):413–436.
10. Stevenson, Harold. "Learning from Asian Schools," 74. Besides this one article, Stevenson has written numerous articles plus with James Stigler, *The Learning Gap.*
11. Ran, An. "Travelling on Parallel Tracks: Chinese Parents and English Teachers." *Educational Research* 43.3 (2001):311–328.
12. Shijun, S. "Models for Bringing up Children. A Literary Approach to the Differences between Chinese and Western Thinking: An Essay." *Childhood* 1 (1993):203–204. The mailing address for the author is given as Su Shijun,

which suggests the journal erred in listing Shijun as the surname. I believe it should be Su, with a given name of Shijun.

13. Li, Jin. "U.S. and Chinese Cultural Beliefs about Learning." *Journal of Educational Psychology* 95.2 (2003):258–267.
14. Li, Jin. "Mind or Virtue: Western and Chinese Beliefs about Learning." *Current Directions in Psychological Science* 14.4 (2005):190–194.
15. Li. "U.S. and Chinese Cultural Beliefs," 265.
16. Li. "Mind or Virtue," 191 and "U.S. and Chinese Cultural Beliefs," 265.
17. Li. "Mind or Virtue," 191.
18. Li and Wang. "Perceptions of Achievement," 413–436.
19. Chua, Amy. *Battle Hymn of the Tiger Mother*. New York: Penguin, 2011.

Chapter 2

1. Sargent, Tanja, and Emily Hannum, "Keeping Teachers Happy: Job Satisfaction among Primary School Teachers in Rural Northwest China." Gansu Survey of Children and Families: Gansu Survey of Children and Families Papers. University of Pennsylvania. 2005, 182–183.
2. Ma, Liping. *Knowing and Teaching Elementary Mathematics: Teachers' Understanding of Fundamental Mathematics in China and the United States.* Mahwah: Erlbaum, 1999, 136.
3. Ding, Weili, and Steven F. Lehrer. "Do Peers Affect Student Achievement in China's Secondary Schools?" *The Review of Economics and Statistics* 89.2 (2007):300–312. Includes a thorough description of the differences between "key" and regular schools.
4. Wang, Xingye. "High School History Education in China and America: A Comparative Study." Final Report of the 2009 Laurence Liu Scholar. (Unpublished.), 2009, 10.
5. Zhao, Yong. "Increasing Math and Science Achievement: The Best and Worst of the East and West." *Phi Delta Kappan* 87.3 (2005):219–222.
6. Wang, Jian, and Lynne W. Paine. "Learning to Teach with Mandated Curriculum and Public Examination of Teaching as Contexts." *Teaching and Teacher Education* 19 (2003):75–94.
7. Stigler, James W. and James Hiebert. "Closing the Teaching Gap." *Phi Delta Kappan* 91.3 (2009):37.
8. Quoted in Sawchuk, Stephen. "Staff Development for Teachers Deemed Fragmented." *Education Week* February 11, 2009, 7. Print.
9. Pine, N. (Ed.). *Participatory Research: Digging Deeper into Classroom Realities.* Teacher Research Series. Claremont, CA: Institute for Education in Transformation, The Claremont Graduate School, 1994.
10. See Cochran-Smith, Marilyn, and Susan L. Lytle. *Inquiry as Stance: Practitioner Research for the Next Generation.* New York: Teachers College, 2009, for an overview of teacher research and its expansion during the last 20 years.
11. Cavanagh, Sean. "Asian Equation." *Education Week* June 6, 2007, 22–26.

12. All children's names are pseudonyms.
13. Louis Carrillo. Interview. June 11, 2011.
14. Wang, Jing. "Curriculum Reform of Elementary Education in China." In China Features, Embassy of the People's Republic of China in the United Kingdom, 2005. Retrieved from http://www.chinese-embassy.org.uk on May 6, 2011 at 2:27 P.M.
15. Sargent, Tanja C. *Institutionalizing Educational Ideologies: Curriculum Reform and the Transformation of Teaching Practices in Rural China.* (Unpublished doctoral dissertation.) University of Pennsylvania, 2006. Retrieved from http://www.ssc.upenn.edu/china/gscf/documents/Sargent_Dissertation.pdf on November 21, 2010.
16. Wang, Xingye. History Education Report, 3.

Chapter 3

1. Bai, Shouyi. *An Outline of History of China.* Beijing: Foreign Languages, 2002.
2. Li, Tianchen, translator. *A Collection of Confucius' Sayings: An English-Chinese Bilingual Textbook.* Jinan, China: Qi Lu Press, 1988, 42.
3. Li. *A Collection of Confucius,* 104.
4. Wang, Robin R. (Ed.). *Images of Women in Chinese Thought and Culture: Writings from the Pre-Qin Period through the Song Dynasty.* Indianapolis: Hackett, 2003, xiv.
5. Li, Jin. "U.S. and Chinese Cultural Beliefs about Learning." *Journal of Educational Psychology* 95.2 (2003):258–267.
6. Li, Jin. "Mind or Virtue: Western and Chinese Beliefs about Learning." *Current Directions in Psychological Science* 14.4 (2005):190–194.
7. Confucius. *The Chinese Classics: Translated into English with Preliminary Essays and Explanatory Notes by James Legge.* Vol. 1. *The Life and Teachings of Confucius.* London: Trubner, 1896. Retrieved from http://oll.libertyfund.org/title/2270/213620 on March 04, 2011.
8. Li. *A Collection of Confucius,* 122.

Chapter 4

1. Stigler, James W., and Harold W. Stevenson. "How Asian Teachers Polish Each Lesson to Perfection." *American Educator* (Spring 1991):12–20, 43–47.
2. Regan, John. Personal Communication. March 3, 1992.
3. Ma, Liping. *Knowing and Teaching Elementary Mathematics: Teachers' Understanding of Fundamental Mathematics in China and the United States.* Mahwah: Erlbaum, 1999.
4. Li, Jun, and Xiaoping Zhao. "Curriculum Design: To Enhance Students' Learning." *ICOTS-7* [International Conference on Teaching Statistics], 2006, 1–6.
5. Li and Zhao. "Curriculum Design," 2.

6. Li and Zhao. "Curriculum Design," 3.
7. Li. "Chinese Teachers' Constructions."

Chapter 5

1. LaFraniere, Suzanne. "China's College Entry Test Is an Obsession." *New York Times* June 16, 2009. Retrieved from http://www.nytimes.com/ 2009/06/13/world/asia/13exam.html on June 13, 2009 at 12:19 P.M.
2. Fairbank, John K., Edwin O. Reischauer, and Albert M. Craig. *East Asia: Tradition & Transformation—New Impression.* Cambridge: Harvard, 1979.
3. Zhang, Qizhi. *Traditional Chinese Culture.* Beijing: Foreign Languages Press, 2004.
4. Spence, Jonathan. *The Search for Modern China.* New York: W. W. Norton, 1991.
5. Zhang. *Traditional Chinese Culture.*
6. Pine, Nancy, and Zhenyou Yu. "Early Literacy Education in China: An Historical Overview." Cynthia B. Leung, and Jiening Ruan (Eds.) *Perspectives on Teaching and Learning Chinese Literacy in China.* Hong Kong: Springer (2012).
7. Yu, Li. "A History of Reading in Late Imperial China, 1000–1800." (Unpublished dissertation.) The Ohio State University, 2003, 61. Retrieved from http://etd.ohiolink.edu/view.cgi?acc_num=osu1054655134 on March 5, 2009.
8. Tsang, Mun C. "Education and National Development in China since 1949: Oscillating Policies and Enduring Dilemmas." *China Review 2000.* Retrieved from http://www.tc.columbia.edu on September 5, 2011.
9. Ministry of Education: The People's Republic of China. "Report of Education Statistics, Volume 1, No. 26, Department of Planning Ministry of Education Feb. 27, 2003." Retrieved from http://www.moe.gov.cn/edas/ website18/en/planning_s.htm on April 27, 2009.
10. Duan, Xin-Ran. "Chinese Higher Education Enters a New Era," *Academe Online.* American Association of University Professors, 2003. Retrieved from http://www.aaup.org/AAUP/pubsres/academe/2003/ND/Feat/duan. htm?PF=1 on April 29, 2009.
11. Wang, Xiufang. *Education in China since 1976.* Jefferson, NC: McFarland, 2003.
12. Ding, Zuyi (Ed.). *Xi'an Fanyi University: Create an Oriental Harvard.* No date. Received shortly after publication in May 2004.
13. Hao, Keqi. Personal Communication. May 7, 2004.
14. Xin, Hao, and Dennis Normile. "Gunning for the Ivy League." *Science* 319 (January 11, 2008):148–151.
15. Li, Huizi, and Wu, Jing. "Thirty Years on, College Entrance Exam Shapes China's Educational Landscape." *Xinhuanet* June 9, 2008. Retrieved from http://news.Xinhuanet.com/English/2008-06/09/content_ 8329989.htm on March 9, 2009.

16. Wang Ruizhe. Interview. June 3, 2011.
17. ACT was formerly American College Testing; ACT is now the official name.
18. Wang Xingye. Interview. June 16, 2010.
19. Jia, David. Personal Communication. May 3, 2006.
20. Jia, David. Personal Communication. May 17, 2006.
21. Pierson, David. "Young, Educated and Jobless in China." *Los Angeles Times* February 19, 2010. Retrieved from http://articles.latime.com/2010/Feb/18/business/la-fi-china-grads19-2010feb19 on February 21, 2010 at 10:13 P.M.
22. Zhou Dandan. Interview. October 21, 2003.
23. Kinzie, Susan. "U.S. Colleges Bask in Surge of Interest among Chinese." *The Washington Post* May 1, 2009. Retrieved from http://www.washingtonpost.com/wp-dyn/content/article/2009/04/30/AR2009043004132.html onMay 10, 2009.
24. Paulson, Amanda. "Record Number of Chinese Students Flock to US Colleges." *The Christian Science Monitor – CSMonitor.Com* November 15, 2010. http://www.csmontior.com/USA/Education/2010/1115 on October 23, 2011 at 11:48 A.M.

Chapter 6

1. Walingsky, Cary. "The Power of Writing." *National Geographic* 196.2 (August 1999):110.

Chapter 7

1. Regional dialects dominate in China, and they vary considerably from one area to the next, sometimes being mutually unintelligible. Young children practice the official dialect of China, *Putonghua* (what Americans call Mandarin), in order to pronounce it accurately.
2. Zhou Dandan. Interview. October 21, 2003.
3. Nancy Pinc. "A Micro-Analysis of Looking Behavior of an English-Speaking and a Chinese-Speaking Child." P. Reich, W. J. Sullivan, and A. R. Lommel (Eds.) *LACUS Forum XXXIII: Variability*. Houston: Linguistic Association of Canada and the United States, 2007, 464–474.
4. Knowles Adkisson. "Malibu High School Subject of Book in China." *The Malibu Times* April 27, 2011. Retrieved from www.malibutimes.com/articles/2011/04/27/news/news5.txt on May 9, 2011.

Chapter 8

1. Harvey, Stephanie, and Anne Goudvis. *Strategies that Work: Teaching Comprehension to Enhance Understanding*. York: Stenhouse, 2000.
2. Sargeant, Tanja C. *Institutionalizing Educational Ideologies: Curriculum Reform and the Transformation of Teaching Practices in Rural China.*

(Unpublished doctoral dissertation.) University of Pennsylvania, 2006. Retrieved from http://www.ssc.upenn.edu/china/gscf/documents/Sargent_Dissertation.pdf on November 21, 2010.

3. Wang, Jing. "Curriculum Reform of Elementary Education in China." In China Features, Embassy of the People's Republic of China in the United Kingdom. Retrieved from http://www.chinese-embassy.org.uk on May 6, 2005 at 2:27 P.M.

4. Rao, Nirmala, and Carol K.K. Chan. "Moving beyond Paradoxes: Understanding Chinese Learners and Their Teachers." Carol K.K. Chan, and Nirmala Rao (Eds.) *Revisiting the Chinese Learner: Changing Contexts, Changing Education.* Hong Kong: Springer, 2009

5. Pine, Nancy, and Zhenyou Yu. "Early Literacy Education in China: An Historical Overview." Cynthia B. Leung, and Jiening Ruan (Eds.) *Perspectives on Teaching and Learning Chinese Literacy in China.* Hong Kong: Springer (2012).

6. Yu, Li. unpublished dissertation. "A History of Reading in Late Imperial China, 1000–1800." The Ohio State University, 2003, 61. Retrieved from http://etd.ohiolink.edu/view.cgi?acc_num=osu1054655134 on November 12, 2005.

7. Yu, Li. "History of Reading," 75–76.

8. Yu. "History of Reading," 78.

9. "Essays." Retrieved from http://professionals.collegeboard.com/testing/sat-reasoning/about/sections/essay on September 21, 2011.

Chapter 9

1. Chinese refer to different dates for major reforms of the 2000s, varying from 1998 to 2002. The cause appears to be that the government issues multiple documents as it engages in reform. It also releases draft documents to be vetted by universities and relevant groups before they are moved into law. In my experience, university professors tend to refer to the earlier dates; elementary and high school administrators refer to the later dates.

2. Zhou, Jun, and Lynda Reed, "Chinese Government Documents on Teacher Education since the 1980s." *Journal of Education for Teaching* 31.3 (2005):212. Also, *Chinese Education and Society* 34:4 2001 excerpts many documents from the 1998–1999 reform flurry.

3. Paine, Lynn W., and Yanping Fang. "Reform as Hybrid Model of Teaching and Teacher Development in China." *International Journal of Educational Research*, 45 (2006):279–289.

4. Yu, Zhenyou. Personal Communication. April 3, 2011.

5. Paine, Lynne W. "The Teacher as Virtuoso: A Chinese Model for Teaching." *Teachers College Record* 92.1 (1990):67.

6. Paine. "Teacher as Virtuoso," 54.

7. Paine, Lynn, and Liping Ma. "Teachers Working Together: A Dialogue on Organizational and Cultural Perspectives of Chinese Teachers." *International Journal of Educational Research* 19.8 (1993):687.

8. Fan Hao, Interview. April 6, 2011.

9. Pine, Nancy, and Zhenyou Yu. "Early Literacy Education in China: An Historical Overview." Cynthia B. Leung, and Jiening Ruan (Eds.) *Perspectives on Teaching and Learning Chinese Literacy in China.* Hong Kong: Springer (2012).

10. Paine and Ma. "Teachers Working Together," 686.

11. Liu Jiantao. Interview. April 9, 2011.

12. Paine and Ma. "Teachers Working Together," 685, and Paine. "Teacher as Virtuoso," 66.

Chapter 10

1. Wang Ruizhe. Interview. June 3, 2011.

2. U.S. Department of Education, National Center for Education Statistics http://nces.ed.gov/programs/digest/d10/tables/dt10_185.asp Tables 36 and 185. Statistics of State School Systems, 1969–1970; Revenues and Expenditures for Public Elementary and Secondary Education, 1979–1980 and 1980–1981; and Common Core of Data (CCD), "National Public Education Financial Survey," 1989–1990 through 2007–2008 (This table was prepared August 2010). Web. September 27, 2011. Retrieved from http://nces.ed.gov/programs/digest/d10/tables/dt10_036.asp September 18, 2011. Source: U.S. Department of Education, National Center for Education Statistics, Common Core of Data (CCD), "State Nonfiscal Survey of Public Elementary/Secondary Education," 1990–1991 through 2008–2009, and Projections of Education Statistics to 2019. (This table was prepared November 2010.) [table 36] Web. September 28, 2011. College Board. "Parents Guide to College." Retrieved from http:/www.collegeboard.com/parents on July 7, 2011.

3. Xu, Jia. "9.33 Million Students Sit the Gaokao." *China Daily USA.* June 7, 2011. Retrieved from http://usa.chinadaily.com.cn/ on June 15, 2011.

4. Hurlbut, Judy. Personal Communication. October 18, 2010.

5. Louis Carrillo. Interview. June 11, 2011.

6. Zhou Dandan. Personal Communication. September 23, 2011.

7. These are the last figures available from both the World Bank and the Chinese government website. The World Bank gives the income that year as $2025; the Chinese government statistics website gives urban income that year as $1609.

8. Fees were obtained from the respective university websites.

9. College Board. "Parents Guide to College." Retrieved from http://www.collegeboard.com/parent/ on July 07, 2011.

10. University of California Los Angeles. "Undergraduate Admissions." Retrieved from http://www.admissions.ucla.edu/Prospect/Adm_fr/FrSel. htm on June 16, 2011 at 12:52 P.M.
11. Amherst College. "Admissions." Retrieved from https://www.amherst.edu/ admission/Amherst on June 16, 2011 at 1:35 P.M.

Chapter 11

1. Vygotsky, Lev S. *Mind in Society: The Development of Higher Psychological Processes.* Cambridge: Harvard University, 1978. Print.
2. Cavanagh, Sean. "Asian Equation." *Education Week* June 6, 2007, 23. Print.
3. Cavanagh, Sean. "Asian Equation," 25.
4. The Ministry of Education and State Council documents of the People's Republic of China are described and quoted in Sargent, Tanja C. *Institutionalizing Educational Ideologies: Curriculum Reform and the Transformation of Teaching Practices in Rural China.* (Unpublished doctoral dissertation.) University of Pennsylvania, 2006, 41–43. Retrieved from www.ssc.upenn.edu/china/gscf/documents/Sargent_Dissertation.pdf. The 1998 document is *Mianshang ershiyi shiji jiaoyu zhenxing xingdong jihua* (Action Plan towards the Revitalization of Education for the 21st Century: People's Republic of China Ministry of Education). The 1999 document is *Guowuyuan guanyu shenhua jiaoyu gaige quanmian tuijin suzhi jiaoyu de jueding* (Decisions of the State Council Regarding the Deepening of Education Reform through the Promotion of Quality Education at all Levels).
5. See previous note.
6. Yang Jin, Interview. April 12, 2011.
7. Fan Hao, Interview. April 6, 2011.
8. Rudowicz, Elisabeth, and Xiao-Dong Yue. "Concepts of Creativity: Similarities and Differences among Mainland, Hong Kong and Taiwanese Chinese." *Journal of Creative Behavior* 34.3 (2000):175–192. Print.
9. Rudowicz and Yue. "Concepts of Creativity," 187.
10. Maisel, Eric. Personal Communication. October 13, 2011.
11. Csikszentmihalyi, Mihaly. *Creativity: Flow and the Psychology of Discovery and Invention.* New York: HarperCollins, 1996.
12. Healy, Jane. *Your Child's Growing Mind: Brain Development and Learning from Birth to Adolescents.* New York: Three River, 2004.
13. Cubba, Stephanie. Personal communication. April 30, 2011.
14. Csikszentmihalyi, Mihaly. *Finding Flow: The Psychology of Engagement with Everyday Life.* New York: Basic Books, 1997, 41.
15. Fawcett, Mary, and Penny Hay. "5x5x5 = Creativity in the Early Years." *The International Journal of Art & Design Education* 23.3 (2004):234–245. Print.
16. Rinaldi, Carlina. *In Dialogue with Reggio Emilia: Listening, Researching, and Learning.* New York: Routledge, 2006.

17. Niu, Weihua, and Robert J. Sternberg. "Societal and School Influences on Student Creativity: The Case of China." *Psychology in the Schools* 40.1 (2003):103–114.

18. Markus, Hazel R., and Shinobu Kitayama. "Culture and the Self: Implications for Cognition, Emotion, and Motivation." *Psychological Review* 98.2 (1991):224–253. Print.

19. Niu and Sternberg. "Student Creativity," 109.

Chapter 12

1. Linda Darling-Hammond. *The Flat World and Education: How America's Commitment for Equity Will Determine Our Future.* New York: Teachers College, 2010, 2.

2. Pujol, Ernesto. "On the Ground: Practical Observations for Regenerating Art Education." *Art School: (Propositions for the 21st Century).* Steven Henry Maddoff (Ed.) Cambridge: MIT, 2009. 1–13.

3. Madoff, Steven Henry. "Introduction." Steven Henry Maddoff (Ed.) *Art School: (Propositions for the 21st Century).* Cambridge: MIT, 2009, ix–xi.

4. Silva, Elena. *Measuring Skills for the 21st Century,* Education Sector Reports, 2008. Retrieved from www.educationsector.org on 26 May 2011.

5. Bransford, J.D., A.L. Drown, and R.R. Cocking (Eds.). *How People Learn,* 2000; OECD, *Innovation in the Knowledge Economy: Implications for Education and Learning,* 2004; and Kozma, R. *Technology, Innovation, and Educational Change: A Global Perspective* Eugene, OR. International Society for Technology in Education, 2003.

6. Wagner, Toni. *The Global Achievement Gap: Why Even Our Best Schools Don't Teach the New Survival Skills Our Children Need—and What We Can Do about It.* New York: Basic Books, 2010, 15.

7. Wagner. *The Global Achievement Gap,* 38–39.

8. Demick, Barbara. "Apple Is Top Banana in China." *Los Angeles Times* October 20, 2011. Retrieved from http://articles.latimes.com/2011/oct/20/world/la-fg-china-apple-20111021 on October 22, 2011.

9. Wang Yan. Interview. April 5, 2011.

10. Jeff Share. Interview. May 17, 2011.

11. Kellner, Douglas, and Jeff Share. "Critical Media Education and Radical Democracy." Michael W. Apple, Wayne Au, and Luis Armando Gandin (Eds.) *The Routledge International Handbook of Critical Education.* New York: Routledge, 2009, 281–95.

12. Share, Jeff. *Media Literacy Is Elementary: Teaching Youth to Critically Read and Create Media.* New York: Peter Lang, 2002.

13. New London Group. "A Pedagogy of Multiliteracies: Designing Social Futures." *Harvard Educational Review,* 66.1 (1966):60–92. Print.

14. Choudhury, Mohammed, and Jeff Share. "Critical Media Literacy: A Pedagogy for New Literacies and Urban Youth." *NCTE Voices in the Middle,* May 2012.

15. International Baccalaureate Programme, IB World School Statistics. Retrieved from http://www.ibo.org on September 28, 2011, 2:21 P.M. http://www.ibo.org.
16. De Orilla a Orilla. Retrieved from http://www.orillas.org on October 17, 2011 at 10:55 A.M.
17. Ketelhut, D. J. "The Impact of Student Self-Efficacy on Scientific Inquiry Skills: An Exploratory Investigation in River City, a Multi-Use Virtual Environment." *The Journal of Science Education and Technology* 16.1 (2007):99–111.
18. IB Programme. Retrieved from http://www.ibo.org on October 7, 2011, 3:35 P.M.
19. Silva. *Measuring Skills for the 21st Century*, 8.
20. U.S. Department of Education, National Center for Education Statistics. Retrieved from http://nces.ed.gov/programs/digest/d10/tables/ Tables 36 and 185.
21. Darling-Hammond, Linda. *The Flat World and Education: How America's Commitment for Equity Will Determine Our Future.* New York: Teachers College, 2010, 324.
22. Darling-Hammond. *The Flat World*, 200.

Bibliography

Adkisson, Knowles. "Malibu High School Subject of Book in China." *The Malibu Times* April 27, 2011. Retrieved from www.malibutimes.com/articles/2011/04/27/news/news5.txt on May 9, 2011.

Amherst College. "Admissions." Retrieved from https://www.amherst.edu/admission/Amherst on June 16, 2011 at 1:35 P.M.

Bai, Shouyi. *An Outline of History of China*. Beijing: Foreign Languages, 2002.

Bransford, J.D., A.L. Brown, and R.R. Cocking (Eds.). *How People Learn*, 2000; OECD, *Innovation in the Knowledge Economy: Implications for Education and Learning*, 2004.

Cavanagh, Sean. "Asian Equation." *Education Week* June 6, 2007, 22–26. Print.

Chan, Carol K.K., and Nirmala Rao (Eds.). *Revisiting the Chinese Learner: Changing Contexts, Changing Education*. Hong Kong: Springer, 2009.

Choudhury, Mohammed, and Jeff Share. "Critical Media Literacy: A Pedagogy for New Literacies and Urban Youth." NCTE *Voices in the Middle*, May 2012.

Chua, Amy. *Battle Hymn of the Tiger Mother*. New York: Penguin, 2011.

Cochran-Smith, Marilyn, and Susan L. Lytle. *Inquiry as Stance: Practitioner Research for the Next Generation*. New York: Teachers College, 2009.

College Board. "Parents Guide to College." Retrieved from http:/www.collegeboard.com/parents on July 7, 2011.

Confucius. *The Chinese Classics: Translated into English with Preliminary Essays and Explanatory Notes by James Legge. Vol. 1. The Life and Teachings of Confucius*. London: Trubner, 1896. Retrieved from http://oll.libertyfund.org/title/2270/213620 on March 04, 2011.

Csikszentmihalyi, Mihaly. *Creativity: Flow and the Psychology of Discovery and Invention*. New York: HarperCollins, 1996.

Csikszentmihalyi, Mihaly. *Finding Flow: The Psychology of Engagement with Everyday Life*. New York: Basic Books, 1997.

Darling-Hammond, Linda. *The Flat World and Education: How America's Commitment for Equity Will Determine Our Future*. New York: Teachers College, 2010.

De Orilla a Orilla. Retrieved from http://www.orillas.org on October 17, 2011 at 10:55 A.M.

Demick, Barbara. "Apple Is Top Banana in China." *Los Angeles Times* October 20, 2011. Retrieved from http://articles.latimes.com/2011/oct/20/world/la-fg-china-apple-20111021 on October 22, 2011.

Ding, Weili, and Steven F. Lehrer. "Do Peers Affect Student Achievement in China's Secondary Schools?" *The Review of Economics and Statistics* 89.2 (2007): 300–312.

Ding, Zuyi (Ed.). *Xi'an Fanyi University: Create an Oriental Harvard.* No date. Received shortly after publication in May 2004. Paper.

Duan, Xin-Ran. "Chinese Higher Education Enters a New Era," *Academe Online.* American Association of University Professors, 2003. Retrieved from http://www.aaup.org/AAUP/pubsres/academe/2003/ND/Feat/duan.htm?PF=1 on April 29, 2009.

"Essays." Retrieved from http://professionals.collegeboard.com/testing/sat-reasoning/about/sections/essay on September 21, 2011.

Fairbank, John K., Edwin O. Reischauer, and Albert M. Craig. *East Asia: Tradition & Transformation—New Impression.* Cambridge: Harvard, 1979.

Fawcett, Mary, and Penny Hay. "5x5x5 = Creativity in the Early Years." *The International Journal of Art & Design Education* 23.3 (2004): 234–245.

Harvey, Stephanie, and Anne Goudvis. *Strategies that Work: Teaching Comprehension to Enhance Understanding.* York: Stenhouse, 2000.

Healy, Jane. *Your Child's Growing Mind: Brain Development and Learning from Birth to Adolescence.* New York: Three Rivers, 2004.

Ingersoll, Richard M. *A Comparative Study of Teacher Preparation and Qualifications in Six Nations.* CPRE Policy Briefs. RB-47. Philadelphia: Consortium for Policy Research in Education, 2007.

International Baccalaureate Programme, IB World School Statistics. Retrieved from http://www.ibo.org on September 28, 2011.

Kellner, Douglas, and Jeff Share. "Critical Media Education and Radical Democracy." Michael W. Apple, Wayne Au, and Luis Armando Gandin (Eds.) *The Routledge International Handbook of Critical Education.* New York: Routledge, 2009, 281–295.

Ketelhut, D.J. "The Impact of Student Self-Efficacy on Scientific Inquiry Skills: An Exploratory Investigation in River City, a Multi-Use Virtual Environment." *The Journal of Science Education and Technology* 16.1 (2007): 99–111.

Kozma, R. *Technology, Innovation, and Educational Change: A Global Perspective.* Eugene, OR: International Society for Technology in Education, 2003.

Kinzie, Susan. "U.S. Colleges Bask in Surge of Interest among Chinese." *The Washington Post* May 1, 2009. Retrieved from http://www.washingtonpost.com/wp-dyn/content/article/2009/04/30/AR2009043004132.html on May 10, 2009.

LaFraniere, Suzanne. "China's College Entry Test Is an Obsession." *New York Times* June 16, 2009. Retrieved from http://www.nytimes.com/2009/06/13/world/asia/13exam.html on June 13, 2009 at 12:19 P.M.

Li, Huizi, and Wu, Jing. "Thirty Years on, College Entrance Exam Shapes China's Educational Landscape." *Xinhuanet* June 9, 2008. Retrieved from http://news.Xinhuanet.com/English/2008–06/09/content_8329989.htm on March 9, 2009.

Li, Jin. "U.S. and Chinese Cultural Beliefs about Learning." *Journal of Educational Psychology* 95.2 (2003): 258–267.

Li, Jin. "Mind or Virtue: Western and Chinese Beliefs about Learning." *Current Directions in Psychological Science* 14.4 (2005): 190–194.

Li, Jin, and Qi Wang. "Perceptions of Achievement and Achieving Peers in U.S. and Chinese Kindergartners." *Social Development* 13.3 (2004): 413–436.

Li, Jun. "Chinese Teachers' Constructions of Their Roles in Developing Curriculum." Paper presented at the 11th International Congress on Mathematical Education (ICME-11), Monterrey, Mexico, 2008. Retrieved from http://dg.icme11.org/tsg/show/18#inner-49 on October 7, 2011.

Li, Jun, and Xiaoping Zhao. "Curriculum Design: To Enhance Students' Learning." *ICOTS-7* [International Conference on Teaching Statistics], 2006, 1–6.

Li, Tianchen, translator. *A Collection of Confucius' Sayings: An English-Chinese Bilingual Textbook*. Jinan, China: Qi Lu Press, 1988.

Ma, Liping. *Knowing and Teaching Elementary Mathematics: Teachers' Understanding of Fundamental Mathematics in China and the United States*. Mahwah: Erlbaum, 1999.

Madoff, Steven Henry. "Introduction." Steven Henry Maddoff (Ed.) *Art School: (Propositions for the 21st Century)*. Cambridge: The MIT Press, 2009, ix–xi.

Markus, Hazel R., and Shinobu Kitayama. "Culture and the Self: Implications for Cognition, Emotion, and Motivation." *Psychological Review* 98.2 (1991): 224–253.

Ministry of Education: The People's Republic of China. "Report of Education Statistics, Volume [sic] 1, No. 26, Department of Planning Ministry of Education Feb. 27, 2003." Retrieved from http://www.moe.gov.cn/edas/website18/en/planning_s.htm on April 27, 2009.

New London Group. "A Pedagogy of Multiliteracies: Designing Social Futures." *Harvard Educational Review* 66.1 (1966): 60–92.

Niu, Weihua, and Robert J. Sternberg. "Societal and School Influences on Student Creativity: The Case of China." *Psychology in the Schools* 40.1 (2003): 103–114.

Paine, Lynne W. "The Teacher as Virtuoso: A Chinese Model for Teaching." *Teachers College Record* 92.1 (1990): 49–81.

Paine, Lynn, and Liping Ma. "Teachers Working Together: A Dialogue on Organizational and Cultural Perspectives of Chinese Teachers." *International Journal of Educational Research* 19(8) (1993): 675–697.

Paine, Lynn W., and Yanping Fang. "Reform as Hybrid Model of Teaching and Teacher Development in China." *International Journal of Educational Research* 45 (2006): 279–289.

Paulson, Amanda. "Record Number of Chinese Students Flock to US Colleges." *The Christian Science Monitor – CSMonitor.Com*. Retrieved from http://www.csmontior.com/USA/Education/2010/1115 on October 23, 2011 at 11:48 A.M.

Pierson, David. "Young, Educated and Jobless in China." *Los Angeles Times* February 19, 2010. Retrieved from http://articles.latime.com/2010/Feb/18/business/la-fi-china-grads19-2010feb19 on February 21, 2010 at 10:13 P.M.

Pine, Nancy. "A Micro-Analysis of Looking Behavior of an English-Speaking and a Chinese-Speaking Child." P. Reich, W. J. Sullivan, and A. R. Lommel (Eds.) *LACUS Forum XXXIII: Variability*. Houston: Linguistic Association of Canada and the United States, 2007, 464–474.

Pine, Nancy (Ed.). *Participatory Research: Digging Deeper into Classroom Realities*. Teacher Research Series. Claremont, CA: Institute for Education in Transformation, The Claremont Graduate School, 1994.

Pine, Nancy, and Zhenyou Yu. "Early Literacy Education in China: An Historical Overview." Cynthia B. Leung, and Jiening Ruan (Eds.) *Perspectives on Teaching and Learning Chinese Literacy in China*. Hong Kong: Springer. (2012)

Pujol, Ernesto. "On the Ground: Practical Observations for Regenerating Art Education." Steven Henry Maddoff (Ed.) *Art School: (Propositions for the 21st Century)*. Cambridge: MIT Press, 2009, 1–13.

Ran, An. "Travelling on Parallel Tracks: Chinese Parents and English Teachers." *Educational Research* 43.3 (2001): 311–328.

Rao, Nirmala, and Carol K.K. Chan. "Moving beyond Paradoxes: Understanding Chinese Learners and Their Teachers." Carol K.K. Chan, and Nirmala Rao (Eds.) *Revisiting the Chinese Learner: Changing Contexts, Changing Education*. Hong Kong: Springer, 2009.

Rinaldi, Carlina. *In Dialogue with Reggio Emilia: Listening, Researching, and Learning*. New York: Routledge, 2006.

Rudowicz, Elisabeth, and Xiao-Dong Yue. "Concepts of Creativity: Similarities and Differences among Mainland, Hong Kong and Taiwanese Chinese." *Journal of Creative Behavior* 34.3 (2000): 175–192.

Sargent, Tanja C. *Institutionalizing Educational Ideologies: Curriculum Reform and the Transformation of Teaching Practices in Rural China*. (Unpublished doctoral dissertation.) University of Pennsylvania, 2006. Retrieved from http://www.ssc.upenn.edu/china/gscf/documents/Sargent_Dissertation.pdf on November 21, 2010.

Sargent, Tanja, and Emily Hannum, "Keeping Teachers Happy: Job Satisfaction among Primary School Teachers in Rural Northwest China." Gansu Survey of Children and Families: Gansu Survey of Children and Families Papers, University of Pennsylvania, 2005, 182–183.

Sawchuk, Stephen. "Staff Development for Teachers Deemed Fragmented." *Education Week* February 11, 2009, 7. Print.

Share, Jeff. *Media Literacy Is Elementary: Teaching Youth to Critically Read and Create Media*. New York: Peter Lang, 2002.

Shijun, S. "Models for Bringing up Children. A Literary Approach to the Differences between Chinese and Western Thinking: An Essay." *Childhood* 1 (1993): 202–211. Print. The mailing address for the author is given as Su

Shijun, which suggests the journal erred in listing Shijun as the surname. I believe it should be Su, with a given name of Shijun.

Silva, Elena. *Measuring Skills for the 21st Century*. Education Sector Reports, 2008. Retrieved from http://www.educationsector.org on May 26, 2011.

Spence, Jonathan. *The Search for Modern China*. New York: W. W. Norton, 1991.

Stevenson, Harold. "Learning from Asian Schools." *Scientific American* December 1992, 70–76.

Stigler, James W., and Harold W. Stevenson. "How Asian Teachers Polish Each Lesson to Perfection." *American Educator* (Spring 1991): 12–20, 43–47.

Stigler, James W., and James Hiebert. "Closing the Teaching Gap." *Phi Delta Kappan* 91.3 (2009): 32–37.

Tang Danlu (Ed.). "Decreased Enrollment Has Chinese Universities Scrambling." *Xinhuanet* June 6, 2011. Retrieved from http://news.xinhuanet.com/english2010/culture/2011–06/06/c_13913482.htm on September 9, 2011, 11:41 A.M.

Tsang, Mun C. "Education and National Development in China since 1949: Oscillating Policies and Enduring Dilemmas." *China Review 2000*. Retrieved from http://www.tc.columbia.edu on September 5, 2011.

University of California Los Angeles. "Undergraduate Admissions." Retrieved from http://www.admissions.ucla.edu/Prospect/Adm_fr/FrSel.htm on June 16, 2011 at 12:52 P.M.

U.S. Department of Education, National Center for Education Statistics. Retrieved from http://nces.ed.gov/programs/digest/d10/tables/dt10_185.asp Tables 36 and 185. Statistics of State School Systems, 1969–1970; Revenues and Expenditures for Public Elementary and Secondary Education, 1979–1980 and 1980–1981; and Common Core of Data (CCD), "National Public Education Financial Survey," 1989–1990 through 2007–2008. (This table was prepared August 2010). Web. Retrieved September 27, 2011. http://nces.ed.gov/programs/digest/d10/tables/dt10_036.asp Source: U.S. Department of Education, National Center for Education Statistics, Common Core of Data (CCD), "State Nonfiscal Survey of Public Elementary/Secondary Education," 1990–1991 through 2008–2009, and Projections of Education Statistics to 2019. (This table was prepared November 2010.) [table 36] Web. Retrieved September 28, 2011.

Vygotsky, Lev S. *Mind in Society: The Development of Higher Psychological Processes*. Cambridge: Harvard University Press, 1978.

Wagner, Toni. *The Global Achievement Gap: Why Even Our Best Schools Don't Teach the New Survival Skills Our Children Need—and What We Can Do about It*. New York: Basic Books, 2010.

Walingsky, Cary. "The Power of Writing." *National Geographic* 196.2 (August 1999): 110–133.

Wang, Jian, and Lynne W. Paine. "Learning to Teach with Mandated Curriculum and Public Examination of Teaching as Contexts." *Teaching and Teacher Education* 19 (2003): 75–94.

Wang, Jing. "Curriculum Reform of Elementary Education in China." In China Features, Embassy of the People's Republic of China in the United Kingdom. Retrieved from http://www.chinese-embassy.org.uk on May 6, 2005 at 2:27 P.M.

Wang, Robin R (Ed.). *Images of Women in Chinese Thought and Culture: Writings from the Pre-Qin Period through the Song Dynasty.* Indianapolis: Hackett, 2003.

Wang, Xiao-lei, Ronan Bernas, and Philippe Eberhard. "Maternal Teaching Strategies in Four Cultural Communities: Implications for Early Childhood Teachers." *Journal of Early Childhood Research* 3.3 (2005): 269–288.

Wang, Xingye. "High School History Education in China and America: A Comparative Study." Final Report of the 2009 Laurence Liu Scholar. (Unpublished.), 2009.

Wang, Xiufang. *Education in China since 1976.* Jefferson, NC:McFarland, 2003.

Xu, Jia. "9.33 Million Students Sit the Gaokao." *China Daily USA* June 7, 2011. Retrieved from http://usa.chinadaily.com.cn/ on June 15, 2011.

Xin, Hao, and Dennis Normile. "Gunning for the Ivy League." *Science* 319 (January 11, 2008): 148–151.

Yu, Li. "A History of Reading in Late Imperial China, 1000–1800." (Unpublished dissertation.) The Ohio State University, 2003. Retrieved from http://etd.ohiolink.edu/view.cgi?acc_num=osu1054655134 on March 5, 2009.

Zhang, Qizhi. *Traditional Chinese Culture.* Beijing: Foreign Languages Press, 2004.

Zhao, Yong. "Increasing Math and Science Achievement: The Best and Worst of the East and West. *Phi Delta Kappan* 87.3 (2005): 219–222.

Zhou, Jun, and Lynda Reed, "Chinese Government Documents on Teacher Education since the 1980s." *Journal of Education for Teaching* 31.3 (2005): 201–213.

Index